22 SUCCESS LESSONS FROM BASEBALL

by
Ron White

Published and distributed by
www.YourSuccessStore.com
2835 Exchange Boulevard
Suite 200
Southlake, Texas 76092
(877)-929-0439

Copyright 2004 Ron White Training
ISBN 0-9747212-0-4
Ron White Training
www.ronwhitetraining.com

22 Success Lessons from Baseball / Ron White

Cover by Envision Works
www.envisionworks.org
Lauren Cleveland

Edited by Julie Neal

Grammar Instruction
Bethe Spurlock

Christy Matthewson Baseball Card Photograph - Old Baseball Card
Photographs, 1887- 1914, www.a2zcds.com
Willie Mays "The Catch", Sandy Koufax - mipakaco-photos
Tinker, Evers, Chance, Steinfield - Trendy Collectibles

We have made every effort to trace the ownership of copyrighted photos.
If we have failed to give adequate credit, we will be pleased to make
changes in future printings.

Printed in the United States

FOREWORD

Take me out to the ball game
Take me out to the crowd
Buy me some peanuts and cracker jacks
I don't care if I never get back

I don't. I don't care if I never get back. That's the truth. What is it about baseball that had me hypnotized at the age of 12; that had my ear glued to a small box of voices that painted a picture of Texas Ranger's baseball? What is it that to this day draws me to the ballpark like nails to a magnet?

I don't know if I can pinpoint it. I don't know if I want to. But, I do know that I love the strategy, the teamwork, the power, the speed, the atmosphere, the sights, the sounds and the smells. I love it all and I'm not alone. The game bears the moniker of our "National Pastime" and I couldn't say it any better.

For me, the quiet time to think is part of the magnetic draw to the game. I love the patience involved for the players, managers and fans. I love pondering the next move in the game, who the manager will substitute, what will the pitcher throw on a 2-1 count or is this the right time
for a bunt?

I know I am biased, but every other sport from my perspective, is simply a way to kill time between baseball seasons. I love to watch the game, study the game, talk to those who love the game and like the old song says, "Root...Root...Root...for the home team!"

By studying baseball, I believe that you can learn a lot about life, success and failure. This book is a collection of short lessons that our national pastime can teach us if we let it. I hope you'll enjoy the book and I look forward to seeing you at the ballpark!

Ron White

TABLE OF CONTENTS

1. Living Legend 7

2. M For Murder 13

3. Wagon Load of Pumpkins 17

4. Nothing To Forgive...............................23

5. Robert Frost And Bobby Thigpen.....................27

6. The Devil Is In The Details.............................33

7. Say It Ain't So 39

8. The Rifle Man 43

9. "I Was As Good As Sandy Koufax" 49

10. Southpaws...55

11. One Thing In Common 59

12. Say Hey...65

13. I'm Gonna Hit It Out 69

14. Cooperstown 73

15. Three Ounces 77

16. Others...81

17. Opening Day 87

18. Control 91

19. Don't Mess With Tex!..............................95

20. Was He Safe?.....................................103

21. Errors That Don't Hurt? 109

22. What's Your Excuse..............................113

23. Baseball Facts 117

24. Strange But True Baseball Injuries.............122

"I'd like to be remembered. I'd like to think that someday two guys will be talking in a bar and one of them will say something like, 'Yeah, he's a good shortstop, but he's not as good as ole Ripken was.'"

Cal Ripken Jr.

LESSON ONE - LIVING LEGEND

Last week I arrived at the ballpark an hour and a half before the game was scheduled to begin. By the time I arrived, the stadium was filled to half capacity. I overheard someone say, "I got here at 1:30." Another proclaimed, "Four o'clock for me."

A young boy had a brand new piece of lumber encased in plastic hoisted above his head. Backpacks were full of balls, pictures, gloves and hats, each eagerly awaiting a chance to be touched and permanently marked by a legend. The aisles were filled with loosely organized lines commencing at the concession stand and coming to an abrupt halt at the barrier between the field and the seats.

They were all here for one man. A man that the fans referred to by first name only. Willie Mays is still Willie Mays, Tony Gwynn is Tony Gwynn and Mark McGwire is still Mark McGwire. However, Cal Ripkin is Cal.

Cal, a man who entered the national pastime at a professional level in 1981, played roughly forty games that year and eeked out a .126 batting average on the season. Twenty years later he announced his exit and assumed his role in baseball immortality. What caused such a stir? Was Cal a home run powerhouse? Not really, he had very good and consistent numbers but wasn't a home run king. His home run total peaked in 1991 with thirty-four home runs that season. Not only was Cal not a home run powerhouse (that typically attracts the spot light), he wasn't a glamorous strike out pitcher either. He was however, a man who unquestionably redefined short stop and what it meant to be a reliable, steady and dedicated baseball player.

Cal wasn't treated as a national treasure when he retired because of his batting average or home runs. Although, these were very admirable statistics he earned during his tenure at shortstop and ones that every baseball player would have been proud to own.

What's the stir all about? You may say, "It's about the streak," but I suggest that it's not. Although Cal's consecutive game streak of 2632 games is one of the most impressive streaks in baseball and all of sports. It's about what *led* to the streak. The stir was about the rare qualities that identified Cal and enabled him to be so consistent for so long. It's about leadership, work ethic and commitment.

These qualities Cal exemplified endeared him to the hearts of baseball fans everywhere. The hard working fans in the stadium seats who couldn't afford to call in sick for work had watched a millionaire refuse to do the same. In doing so, Cal personified what is good about America, about hard work and being faithful to your task even when you don't feel like it. Cal played with a broken nose after a freak accident in an All Star Game photograph. The steel mill workers, auto assembly line men, coal miners, police officers and construction workers embraced Cal because he lived a life that they lived – only on a grander stage.

So there I was, watching the Texas Rangers and Baltimore Orioles face each other in a game that had no merit other than the fact that Cal was playing his last game in Arlington. When Cal came to bat for the first time in the game, he received a standing ovation. Sure, baseball players receive standing ovations all the time. The unique thing about this ovation was the zip code. It was Arlington--Arlington, Texas that is. Not Baltimore, Maryland. This ovation was for a man who hadn't even swung the bat yet.

As I sat at the game, I stared in awe of Cal for nine innings. Somewhere in the middle innings I realized that you don't have to be flashy or have power numbers to be great. It's about the simple things that are the hard things. It's about leadership, work ethic and commitment. I seem to find myself wanting the glory, wanting the home runs, grand slams and power, but, when it comes down to it, that isn't what it's all about. Thanks for reminding me, Cal.

ACTION POINTS

1. Who do you admire?

2. List at least three qualities about them that you admire:
   a.

   b.

   c.

3. Are these the priorities you work hard to achieve daily?

4. How do the priorities you chase differ from the ones you truly admire in others?

5. How should you shift your priorities?

"I know, but I had a better year than Hoover."

> *Babe Ruth's response when a*
> *reporter pointed out that*
> *Ruth made more money*
> *than President Hoover*

"It was so wonderful, Joe. You have never heard such cheering."... "Yes, I have."

> *Conversation between Marilyn Monroe*
> *and Joe DiMaggio. Marilyn had just*
> *entertained 100,000 troops in Korea*

"After the series, the league above the Major Leagues will draft Orel Herscheiser as number one."

> *Mike Marshall, after Orel shutout*
> *Oakland and got three hits*
> *Himself in Game 2*
> *of the 1988 World Series*

"If a woman has to choose between catching a fly ball and saving an infant's life, she will always choose saving an infant's life without even considering if there are men on base."

> *Unknown*

"When I was a small boy in Kansas, a friend of mine and I went fishing. I told him that I wanted to be a real Major League baseball player, a genuine professional like Honus Wagner. My friend told me that he would like to be President of the United States. Neither of us got our wish."

> *Dwight D. Eisenhower*

"I was a nervous wreck out there. Swear to God. I felt like I was in the presence of the President."

> *Mariners reserve catcher John Marzano,*
> *after hitting a double and winding up*
> *standing next to Baltimore's Cal Ripken Jr.*

"On turf the ball comes to me and says, 'Catch me.' On grass it says, 'Look out, sucker.'"

> *Greg Pryor*

"Well, you can't win them all!"

> *Connie Mack on his 1916 A's*
> *who went 36-117*

"People ask me how I'd like to be remembered. I tell them I would like to be remembered as the one who hit the line drive over Bobby Richardson's head."

> *Willie McCovey who ended game seven of the 1962*
> *World Series with a liner caught by Bobby Richardson*

"A full mind is an empty bat."

> *Branch Rickey*

"The other day they asked me about mandatory drug testing. I said 'I believed in drug testing a long time ago. All through the '60's I tested everything.'"

> *Bill Lee*

"I don't like to sound egotistical, but every time I stepped up to the plate with a bat in my hands, I couldn't help but feel sorry for the pitcher."

> *Rogers Hornsby*

"In 1962 I was named Minor League Player of the Year. It was my second season in the Bigs."

> *Bob Uecker*

"Nobody goes there... it's too crowded."
Yogi Berra

Quotes by Willie Mayes

"Every time I look at my pocketbook, I see Jackie Robinson."

"I don't compare 'em, I just catch 'em."

"If you can do that - if you run, hit, run the bases, hit with power, field, throw and do all other things that are part of the game – then you're a good ballplayer."

"I think I was the best baseball player I ever saw."

"It's not hard. When I'm not hitting, I don't hit nobody. But when I'm hitting, I hit anybody."

"They throw the ball, I hit it. They hit the ball, I catch it."

LESSON TWO - M FOR MURDER

Ruth and Gehrig, Gehrig and DiMaggio, DiMaggio and
Keller and Mantle and Maris. The New York Yankees began
a tremendous sports dynasty in the 1920's and have created a
mystique that lasts until this day. There is no middle ground
with the Yankees for baseball fans. They are either held close
to the heart and loved, or despised as a villain to be defeated
season after season. Throughout their celebrated history, they
have possessed some phenomenal tandems, and none have
been more lethal than Mantle and Maris. The press in New
York was giddy at the thought of Mantle and Maris in the
heart of the pin-stripped lineup. The press dubbed this duo
"Dial M for Murder" and "Maul and Mangle."

How good would Ruth have been without Gehrig? Most
likely, he'd still be phenomenal. Lou Gehrig would still be the
"Iron Man" without DiMaggio. DiMaggio would have still
made pitchers legs weak without Keller. Mantle did not
possess such great talents because of his association with
Maris. He would have been a star anyway. However, there is
no discounting what tandems like these do to a pitcher. These
are the kind of back to back batters that pitchers have
nightmares about. Who can you pitch around?

To the casual baseball observer they may not notice the
impact of tandems on a pitcher. In the 2000 baseball season,
in St. Louis, Jim Edmonds was tearing up the baseball world
once again with his unbelievable statistics. Then Mark
McGwire, his "protection" in the line up went down with an
injury and Edmonds batted .100 points lower for the rest of
the season. You see, with McGwire's injury, the need to
throw Edmonds a quality pitch declined.

Why would a pitcher throw a strike to Edmonds, Mantle or
Griffey if the next guy hitting was an easier out? The theory

is to throw the superstar borderline pitches that very easily may lead to a walk. The pitcher knows that he can put him on base with a free pass and then focus his attention on the easier out. After all, that is much more desirable than serving up a home run and then facing the "lesser" batter.

The strategy works on many occasions. However, when the man coming up next is also a powerhouse, you can't do that. You can't give him the opportunity to hit with a man on base. It could turn into an RBI situation very quickly. So, what do you do? You have to throw strikes. This gives the pitcher the opportunity to get the first superstar out and avoid pitching to the second with a man on base. However, this also gives the batter an opportunity to add to his statistics.

Sure, you can be great as a Lone Ranger. You can be a standout and the one shining light on a miserable team. But, those who are really great are that way because they are surrounded with greatness.

Go out of your way to surround yourself with greatness. It will only make you better. In the business world, smart managers will hire smart people. However, a really smart manager will hire those smarter than himself. Don't fear that you have to squash the accomplishments of those around you to make yourself appear great. Make yourself great by supporting the success of others.

ACTION POINTS

1. Do you make those around you better?

2. Do you surround yourself with those who are better in your arena than you are?

3. If not, what can you do to surround yourself with those better than you?

4. Remember that you can't do it alone. Standing next to greatness won't diminish you. It will make you better. Share the success and the success will be greater.

Quotes from Mike Schmidt

"Any time you think you have the game conquered, the game will turn around and punch you right in the nose."

"I could ask the Phillies to keep me on to add to my statistics, but my love for the game won't let me do that."

"I don't think I can get into my deep inner thoughts about hitting. It's like talking about religion."

"If you could equate the amount of time and effort put in mentally and physically into succeeding on the baseball field and measured it by the dirt on your uniform, mine would have been black."

"Pete Rose is the most likable arrogant person I've ever met."

"If you're associated with the Philadelphia media or town, you look for negatives. I don't know if there's something about their upbringing or they have too many hoagies, or too much cream cheese."

"They read their sports pages, know their statistics and either root like hell or boo our butts off. I love it. Give me vocal fans, pro or con, over the tourist types who show up in Houston or Montreal and just sit there."

LESSON THREE - WAGON LOAD OF PUMPKINS

In 1973, a frustrated manager was asked about his struggling rookie third baseman. He said, "I would trade him for a wagon load of pumpkins!" You might surmise that this third baseman didn't make his mark on baseball history. A good guess would be that he was out of the Major Leagues by the end of the year and today you can find him painting white divider stripes on roads for $7.25 per hour.

Let's take a step back. The above assumptions are natural ones after hearing that his manager would trade him for a "wagon load of pumpkins." After hearing the statement you could draw one of two conclusions. Either this was a really bad baseball player or this manager had a major craving for pumpkin pie.

Neither of the conclusions would be correct. The manager was Danny Ozark and the third baseman was referred to by his teammates as "Schmitty." You may know him as Mike Schmidt. Yes...that Mike Schmidt. He played for 18 seasons and slammed 548 home runs. He accumulated 1,595 RBI's, led the Phillies to five divisional championships, a pennant and a World Series victory. Yet, his rookie year he couldn't hit Major League pitching to save his life. He batted .196 that year with 136 strikeouts in just 367 at bats.

Mike Schmidt didn't win rookie of the year awards, but the remaining 17 years of his career rank with the best in baseball. Schmidt was a player who was confident in his abilities. His rookie year he struck out four times in one game to Tom Seaver. After the game, Mike said the at bats were "comfortable." He reasoned that he just "swung through" the ball. Now, that's having a positive attitude and believing in yourself even when you are the only one.

Schmidt's story could have so easily been like many others in the game of life. All too often when we don't see immediate results we quit and move on to the next venture. If at first we don't succeed...we quit. Schmidt wasn't a quitter and despite Ozark's remarks about pumpkins, neither was his manager. They pursued their goal of making Mike an All- Star and they succeeded big time.

It has been said that, "Life is not what happens to you, but what you do with what happens to you." Many people have a victim mentality and when they are confronted with obstacles, they give up and make excuses coupled with complaints about their lot. Schmidt didn't give up or complain. He persisted in his goal.

Thomas Edison constructed over 1,000 light bulbs before he found one that worked. A reporter asked him, "Mr. Edison, how does it feel to have failed over 1,000 times?" To which he promptly replied, "I didn't fail 1,000 times, I successfully found 1,000 ways that the light bulb would not work!" I am sure that Edison and Schmidt would tell you to learn from your mistakes, don't let them consume you and press on towards your goal.

Overnight successes rarely occur overnight. Without patience and an unrelenting grasp of your goals, you may end up as another statistic. Mike, thank you for your perseverance, for the memories and Philadelphia thanks you for the pennants. By the way Mr. Ozark, could you pass a piece of pumpkin pie?

ACTION POINTS

1. In the areas of your life that are the most important to you, what results are you currently getting?

2. Are you willing to pursue your goal despite setbacks?

3. Have you given up on a goal that you would like to pick back up? It's not too late, be specific.

4. Is your dream real, clear, and precise?

5. Write down the rewards of the met goal.

   a.
   b.
   c.
   d.

6. Write down the steps necessary to accomplish this goal.

   a.
   b.
   c.
   d.

Quotes From Yogi Berra

"You can't think and hit at the same time."

"A nickel ain't worth a dime anymore."

"The only reason I need these gloves is cause of my hands."

"We were overwhelming underdogs."

"The other team could make trouble for us if they win."

"It's never happened in World Series history, and it hasn't happened since."

"It's deja-vu all over again!"

"We made too many wrong mistakes."

"If people don't come to the ballpark, how are you gonna stop them?"

"If you ask me a question I don't know I'm not going to answer."

"Slump? I ain't in no slump... I just ain't hitting."

"It was hard to have a conversation with anyone, there were too many people talking."

"I'll say this much for baseball...it's beyond question the greatest conversation piece ever invented in America."

Bruce Catton, Fascinating Baseball Facts

"A hot dog at the ball park is better than a steak at the Ritz."
Humprey Bogart in an organized film for baseball

"The game of baseball is a clean, straight game and it summons to its presence everybody who enjoys clean, straight athletics. It furnishes amusement to the thousands and thousands."
William Howard Taft

"The secret to managing is keeping the guys who hate you away from the guys who are undecided."
Casey Stengel

"People ask me what I do in winter when there is no baseball. I will tell you what I do, I stare out the window and wait for spring."
Rogers Hornsby

"To try to sneak a fastball past Hank Aaron is like trying to sneak a sunrise past a rooster."
Joe Adock

"Pro-rated at 500 at bats per year, my 1,081 strike outs would mean that for 2 years out of the fourteen that I played, I never touched the ball."
Norm Cash

"I am tired of it. I don't want to hear about it anymore."
Bill Buckner

"You're trying your damnedest, you strike out and they boo you. I act like it doesn't bother me, like I don't hear anything the fans say, but the truth is I hear every word of it and it kills me."
Mike Schmidt

LESSON FOUR - NOTHING TO FORGIVE

This one is for Mitch Williams, Bill Buckner, Ralph Branca, Donnie Moore and every Cub since World War II. It's for the '64 Phillies, the '78 Red Sox and the '87 Blue Jays. It's for all the players who attempted great things and fell short. It's for those who risked failure and dared to appear inept, clumsy and foolish. It's for every "goat" that accomplished more than 99.9% of those in their field and are chided as failures.

The "Wild Thing" Mitch Williams trotted in from the bullpen to shutdown the Toronto Blue Jays and seal the World Series victory for the Phillies. Instead, he served up the game winning home run to Joe Carter and broke the hearts of everyone in Philadelphia. Williams received death threats. Bill Buckner failed to stop a ball from rolling through his legs in 1986 and will forever be remembered as the man who squandered Boston's World Series dreams. Bill was asked if he considered suicide after his error. What kind of person asks this question? As far-fetched as that question sounds, Donnie Moore did commit suicide.

Donnie Moore was the California Angels pitcher who gave up the game winning home run to Dave Henderson in the 1986 American League playoffs that allowed Boston to advance to the World Series. He had a two-strike count on Henderson and was one pitch away from the victory and the Series when he threw that final pitch. No one will be able to prove that this episode is what led Moore to shoot his wife and then himself. Although, those that know him best say that was the catalyst. The beginning of the end.

"Ever since he gave up the home run...he was never himself again," said Dave Pinter, Moore's agent for twelve years. "He blamed himself for the Angels not going to the World Series.

He constantly talked about the Henderson home run...I tried to get him to go to a psychiatrist. But he said, 'I don't need it...I'll get over it.'...that home run killed him." The former Angel, Brian Downing, echoed the sentiment by simply saying, "You destroyed a man's life over one pitch."

If we were honest with ourselves, we would admit that we are not on the field with these men because they have talents, skills and abilities we don't have. They are there because they have a discipline we don't have and they are willing to risk failure for the small chance of great success. Yet, we chide and harass them for their failure as if they have disgraced our team, city and families, when in reality, they are the best of the best. If there is a beginning there is an end. If there is a winner there must be a loser. It's as simple as that. Although, all too often, we stand indignant, unrelenting and unforgiving. Let me say it once and for all. Bill Buckner, Donnie Moore, Mitch Williams, Johnny Pesky, Tom Niedenfuer and every other unfairly criticized player, the reason we don't forgive you is there is nothing to forgive. Nothing at all. You dared to stand in the arena. You dared to stand in the winner's circle in the midst of grand circumstances and fell short because someone had to.

What prompts a person to be critical of another? Is this admonishing intended for good or is it vindictive? The kind of criticism that finds its origins in an effort to belittle another person because of their failure only brings an unwelcome light to the dark closet of their own insecurity. The men and women who risk and fail are indeed far better off than those who stand outside of the fire. Herman Melville said, "He who has never failed somewhere, that man cannot be great." The man who sits in the stands of life will be sentenced to an existence of unrealized dreams. The individual who dares to suit up and then fails, has already succeeded.

Teddy Roosevelt tells us that the true failure is "The cold and timid souls who know neither victory nor defeat." Thank you for knowing defeat. Thank you for risking. No, you are not forgiven. There is nothing to forgive.

Action Points

1. Are you a critical person?

2. When you criticize others for failing, what does that say about you?

3. Are you afraid to fail?

4. Are you leading a challenging life? What can you do today to risk failure?

5. What is your dream?

6. Pursue your dream. Falling short is not failure. Failure is inaction.

7. Watch how you criticize others. Remember that a secure person sees no need to tear others down.

8. Finally, when you are criticized by those standing on the side lines, notice where they are standing...the sidelines.

Thomas Boswell wrote an article titled "Nothing To Forgive" that was included in his 1990 collection "Game Day" and was the inspiration for this lesson. Thank you, Thomas. You are a true baseball fan.

"Nothing flatters me more than to assume that I could write prose-unless it be to have it assumed that I once pitched a baseball with distinction."
Robert Frost

"You don't save pitchers for tomorrow. Tomorrow it might rain."
Leo Durocher

"That just shows you how this league has gone to hell."
Chuck Finley on his selection as
American League Player of the week

"The music sounds better, the wine tastes sweeter and the girls look better when we win."
Mark Grace

"The difference between the old ballplayer and the new ballplayer is the jersey. The old ballplayer cared about the name on the front. The new ballplayer cares about the name on the back."
Steve Garvey

"You spend a good piece of your life gripping a baseball and in the end it turns out that it was the other way around all the time."
Jim Bouton

"I don't want to embarrass any other catcher by comparing him to Johnny Bench."
Sparky Anderson

Lesson Five - Robert Frost and Bobby Thigpen

Bobby Thigpen spent most of his career with the Chicago White Sox and had a good baseball career. However, I am sure that it's a little known fact that he also fancied himself as somewhat of a poet. That's right... a poet. The man who the White Sox looked to in the ninth to mow down batters could have been the next Robert Frost.

Actually, that may be an exaggeration. His poetry most likely would not have received an "A" in any junior high English class. Thigpen, after his first full year in the Major Leagues, posted a 7 and 5 record with 16 saves and an ERA of 2.70. But, he did sense that the possibility of not being signed was real. He sent this short poem to White Sox chairman Jerry Reinsdorf:

> As I sit at home this off-season,
> I wonder what the hell is the reason,
> Why the club wants to be unfair,
> Underpaying a player who can produce and care.

Reinsdorf could roll with the punches and promptly responded with some rhymes of his own.

> I hope you are a really good pitcher,
> Because as a poet you will never get richer;
> If you are not pitching this year,
> I will be sad but won't fear;
> Though you may be one of the best,
> There's always someone among the rest.

At this point it was getting fun. And Thigpen couldn't resist but to respond with more poetry of his own. Thigpen sent this gem to his fellow poet:

It is true that my potential as a poet is very small,
But, in the ninth who do you want to have the ball?
You say there will always be someone among the rest,
But, who do you want, them or the best?

Thigpen didn't get his salary doubled like he wanted, but he did get signed and had a nice career. Someone once said, "Life is too serious to be taken seriously." Thigpen is a man who had an unconventional and fun approach to a very serious issue, such as his salary. How often in business and life do you make a serious situation only more serious by being unnecessarily stoic? If we can learn any lesson from Thigpen it would be to lighten up and have some fun.

Action Points

1. Be creative!!!

2. Have fun. Life is too serious to be taken seriously.

3. Is there someone you have been unsuccessful at getting an appointment or meeting with?

4. How can you have some fun and be creative to accomplish your goal?

"He wants Texas back."
Tommy Lasorda, Dodger manager, was
asked what terms Mexican-born pitching
sensation Fernando Valenzuela might settle for
in his upcoming contract negotiations in 1981

"It's a beautiful day for a night game."
Announcer Frankie Frisch

"It was too bad I wasn't a second baseman; then I'd probably
have seen a lot more of my husband."
Karolyn Rose, ex-wife of Pete Rose, 1981

"The Oakland Athletics are 32-0 in games in which they have
scored more runs than their opponents."
According to the Chicago Tribune, this statistic was given in
the press notes for a Chicago-Oakland game

"I watch a lot of baseball on the radio."
President Gerald Ford, 1978

"I won't play for a penny less than fifteen hundred dollars."
Honus Wagner, turning down an offer of $2,000.

After being snubbed from the All-Star game by Boston
manager, Darrell Johnson, Baltimore's Jim Palmer claimed he
was misquoted for calling Johnson an idiot. "I did not call
Johnson an idiot. Someone else did and I just agreed," Palmer
said.

"This is a tough ballpark for a hitter when the air conditioner
is blowing in."
Bob Boone on the Houston Astrodome

"I am the most loyal player money can buy."
Don Sutton, player for the Astros,
Dodgers, Brewers, Athletics and Angels
"Ninety feet between the bases is the nearest thing to perfection that man has yet to achieve."
Red Smith

"Man may penetrate the outer reaches of the universe, he may solve the very secret of eternity itself but for me, the ultimate human experience is to witness the flawless execution of the hit and run."
Branch Rickey

"Baseball is a game yes. It is also a business. But what it is most truly is disguised combat. For all its gentility, its leisurely pace, baseball is violence under wraps."
Willie Mays

"There have been only two geniuses in the world, Willie Mays and Willie Shakespeare."
Tallulah Bankhead

"I'd walk through hell in a gasoline suit to keep playing baseball."
Pete Rose

"We are on a first number basis with each other. He calls me 3 and I call him 2."
Bill Lee

1907 CHICAGO CUBS WORLDS CHAMPS INFIELD

H.STEINFELDT (3B)   J.TINKER (SS)   J.EVERS (2B)   F.CHANCE (1B)

LESSON SIX - THE DEVIL IS IN THE DETAILS

The year was 1908 and the Cubs were playing the Giants. On that day one of the most bizarre plays in baseball history took place. The New York Giants fans stormed the field celebrating what they believed to be their victory over the Cubs. While at the same time, Johnny Evers and Joe Tinker of the Cubs were wrestling with third base coach, Joe McGinnity, for the ball that was still in play despite the celebration.

The next thing you know, Tinker throws the ball in the stands and Cub pitcher Floyd Kroh gallops into the crowd and hits a fan on the head to get the ball back. Perhaps I should take a step back, Johnny Evers was the second baseman for the Cubs and runners were on the corners. There were two outs and the score was tied. The batter, McCormick, singled to center and the run from third scored. The fans went nuts! They began pouring in from the stands. Johnny Evers, the second baseman, was watching the runner from first, Merkle, who saw the fans come on the field and stopped half way on his way to second. He began the celebration with the rest of his team.

Johnny Evers ran to get the ball but the third base coach for the Giants was watching Evers and got wise to his idea. He wrestled the ball away and tossed it into the stands. Then Cub pitcher, Floyd Kroh, leaped into the stands and pleaded with the fan to give the ball back for "just a minute." The fan refused so Kroh hit him on the head and the ball was dropped. Kroh picked up the ball and threw it to second where the umpire and Evers were patiently waiting. Evers caught the ball and tagged the bag and the umpire quietly said to Evers, "That run does not count." The umpire then walked off the field and made no attempt to continue the game in the confusion. It was later replayed and the Cubs won because of what was referred to as "Merkle's Boner." What a crazy series of events. Could you imagine Derek Jeter hitting a fan to get a ball back? Definitely one of the most unique plays in Major League history. But, what led to the play? The reason that the play occurred the way it did was the lack of follow through and attention to detail of the runner on first. He didn't finish his job. He didn't complete his assigned chore. That chore was to simply touch second base. How many times do you complete a task 90% at the office or home and you think no one is watching? Someone is always watching, even if that someone is only you.

I have a good friend who used to drive a shuttle bus for a five-star hotel. One day, business guru, Steve Forbes, was in his shuttle. My friend seized the moment and asked him, "If you could share just one piece of advice with me in regards to business what would it be?" Steve leaned forward and without a moments hesitation said, "Details. The devil is in the details." It most definitely is. If you are a big picture person and not good with details then get someone on your team who is, because "The Devil is in the details." Just ask Merkle.

If your function in your organization is to set the course for your team, then do so. When setting this path, as a leader, make sure everyone knows the big picture or ultimate goal. Remind them of it often to avoid prolonged discouragement. However, with one eye on the goal make sure the other eye is focused on the details. If this is not possible for you, then get someone who can focus on the details. This person may not get the glory in the organization. But, you will know their role and make sure they are appreciated. They are the irreplaceable cog in the wheel of success. "Details, details, details. The devil is in the details." The most incredible accomplishment may crumble before solidified because of inattention to details.

Action Points

1. Are you a detail-oriented person?

2. If you are, are there areas that you are not delivering 100%? What are they?

3. If you are not, whom can you bring in to assist you in the details while you remain focused on the big picture?

4. In your business and personal life is every penny accounted for? Be honest and specific. What can you do to make sure that it is?

5. Are there tensions that are not addressed? A hairline crack in a 747, if not addressed, will destroy the lives of hundreds.

6. Are your bills paid on time?

7. Evers paid attention to details. His team eventually won the game because of it.

Quotes from Dan Quisenberry

"A manager uses a relief pitcher like a six shooter, he fires until it's empty then takes the gun and throws it at the villain."

"He (Ted Simmons) didn't sound like a baseball player. He said things like 'nevertheless' and 'if, in fact.'"

"I found a delivery in my flaw."

"It (his contract) has options through the year 2020 or until the last Rocky movie is made."

"I thought (while batting) they were in a zone, but they were playing man to man."

"I've seen the future and it's much like the present only longer."

"I want to thank (winning the '82 Fireman award) all the pitchers who couldn't go nine innings and manager Dick Howser who wouldn't let them go."

"Natural grass is a wonderful thing for little bugs and sinkerball pitchers."

"Our fielders have to catch a lot of balls, or at least deflect them to someone who can."

Quotes from Pete Rose

"Am I still in uniform? Then I ain't retired."

"Doctors tell me I have the body of a thirty-year-old. I know I have the brain of a fifteen-year-old. If you've got both, you can play baseball."

"(Don) Gullett's the only guy who can throw a baseball through a car wash and not get the ball wet."

"How can anyone as slow as you (Tony Perez) pull a muscle?"

"I haven't missed a game in two-and-a-half years. I go to the park as sick as a dog and when I see my uniform hanging there, I get well right away. Then I see some of you guys (media) and I get sick again."

"I'm just like everybody else. I have two arms, two legs and four thousand hits."

"I told him (Pete Rose, Jr.) who to watch. I said if you want to be a catcher, watch Johnny Bench. If you want to be a right-handed power hitter, watch Mike Schmidt. If you just want to be a hitter, watch me."

"Sure I do, and if someone paid you six-thousand dollars a game, you'd have fun as well."

Lesson Seven - Say It Ain't So

It started as a few gamblers scheming to get rich and concluded as easily one of the darkest days in baseball history. The thirty-seventh President of the United Sates once said, 'The game of baseball is a clean, straight game.' Yet, the actions of a handful of Chicago White Sox in 1919 left a stain on the game that many believed, at the time, would be too hard for the sport to overcome. Fortunately, baseball did recover and has seen nothing close to this scandal since - and it has marched on to become our national pastime.

The tragedy of the 1919 Black Sox scandal, as it was soon to become known, lies in the evidence that at least seven and potentially eight members of the Chicago White Sox violated the trust of the fans and the integrity of the game. It began because a small number of gamblers wanted to hit the jackpot and figured the easiest way to do it was to ensure it with a fix.

When aiming to uncover the mastermind of the fix; you won't be able to find a single ring leader. Instead it was a work of collaboration fueled by greed. Two men, however, stand out above the rest: William Thomas "Sleepy Bill" Burns and Billy Maharg. Burns used to play in the Major Leagues and thus had connections with the players. Maharg was the gambler with the connections underground. These two men approached two of the White Sox players, Pitcher Ed Cicotte and First Baseman Arnold "Chick" Gandil, about fixing the Series with the promise of a year's salary as the reward.

All in all, this group of underground gamblers bet almost one million dollars on the series and the Reds to win it. Eight players went along with the fix – pitcher Ed Cicotte, first baseman Arnold "Chick" Gandil, pitcher Lefty Williams, centerfielder Happy Felsch, shortstop Swede Risberg, third baseman Buck Weaver, utility man Fred McMullin, and one of the best and most popular stars ever, leftfielder "Shoeless" Joe Jackson. Although Joe Jackson held to his dying day that he was innocent and at the end of his life even proclaimed, 'I am now going to the greatest umpire of them all – and He knows I am innocent.' It seems that Jackson could have been innocent. In the Series, he hit a robust .375 while setting a major league World Series record with 12 hits, one of which was the only home run hit during the entire Series – not quite the mark of a man throwing a series. Moreover, evidence says he knew of the fix and asked to be benched because of it - but that offering was overruled.

Whether Jackson was guilty or not, many others definitely were and that was enough to fracture the soul of the game... at least for a moment. The problem with a fix this big was that it required many collaborators and that meant lots of talking. It has been said that loose lips sink ships, and loose lips certainly sunk this illegal operation.

Reading about the 1919 World Series is almost like watching your favorite team getting slaughtered by the team that you hate. You turn the television off because it's too hard to watch. That team is greed. The members of the 1919 White Sox were human, and by that definition, they will have shortcomings, failures and imperfections. By that definition they are mortal, just like every other person who has ever lived. This perhaps explains the actions of greed that took place on that baseball diamond so many years ago, yet it does not come close to excusing them. We are all faced with temptations and opportunities for an easy mark every day.

Sometimes we will give in and sometimes we won't. The challenge is to develop who you are to the point that when life approaches you with an under-the-table offer, you reflexively turn the other way.

Character counts and it's important. It's not just great accomplishments that make someone great. It's those accomplishments coupled with character and integrity. Every year a national poll places Billy Graham as the most respected man in the nation. Even men and women who do not share his faith place him at the top of the list. It's because of his character and integrity. These intangible and often overlooked qualities do count.

If your hand is in the cookie jar...get it out. Get it out right now. If you do it now, perhaps only you and your conscience will have to resolve this issue. However, eventually every stink finds its way to the surface. Trying to cover scandal and wrong is like attempting to build a pyramid out of birdseed. It won't work. It's just a matter of time before you will be discovered. Even if the discovery isn't public, your conscience will discover it and haunt you until you are calloused to the evil. Then you have really lost.

To the team of 1919 I say, you are no different than me in that you are flawed. My flaws have not been exposed to the entire world. The ones that have been exposed are known only to my small world of people. Your accomplishments are awesome and it's hard for me to read about your fall from the baseball pedestal. But, this baseball fan has taken a lesson from you. Character and integrity do count.

Please say it ain't so…

Action Points

1. What are you weaknesses?

2. How could these weaknesses adversely affect your life?

3. Is your hand in the cookie jar? If it's, get it out right now. No exceptions and no rationalizing. Put down this book and do it right now.

4. Is there anyone you know that you can be honest with and they can hold you accountable for avoiding this behavior?

5. Watch yourself on even the little things. Integrity counts and being consistent with a lot of little things adds up to big things.

LESSON EIGHT - THE RIFLE MAN

The adolescent Johnny Crawford referred to him as "pa" on the western television series "The Rifle Man." Chuck Connors played the towering, honest, sharp shooting rancher named Lucas McCain. I never ceased to marvel at how Chuck would save his entire town from the weekly outlaw by simply twirling his rifle on his finger and placing one or two perfectly placed bullets in his target.

Not everyone knows that before Chuck began his career as a television star he was a first baseman for the Chicago Cubs and Brooklyn Dodgers. When he played for the Dodgers, the owner was a man named Branch Rickey. Rickey was a very religious and moral man. He was also extremely tight with a dollar and seldom paid more than necessary to any player or team.

Very few people outsmarted the sharp Rickey in negotiations. However, it should be no surprise that the same man, who weekly outsmarted villains attempting to disrupt the old-west ranching community of Norfolk, also got the best of Rickey. It was time for salary negotiations, and in those days the players often did their own negotiating. It was sometimes a nervous and gut-wrenching experience, especially when it was with Rickey.

Gene Hermanski met with Rickey first. Connors sought out Hermanski and asked him how the meeting went. Hermanski did not fare well in his negotiation process and said, "He asked me if I drank and I told him 'only socially' so he refused to give me a raise." Connors filed that piece of information in his mental data banks and strolled into Rickey's office. During the course of the meeting Rickey asked him his moralistic question. Connors promptly replied, "Mr. Rickey, if I have to drink to be a part of this team...I don't want to be any part of it."

The pleased Rickey smiled and "The Rifle Man" received his raise by using the same wit he defended the town of Norfolk with. Connors did his homework before he went into the meeting. As basic as it sounds, many sales people will go into a sales presentation without anticipating objections and therefore will have no answers to overcome them. Sometimes business professionals decide that they can just "wing it" in an important meeting and be successful. Or in our personal lives we do not prepare for our days and just let them happen around us.

Harvey Mackay wrote a book titled, "Swim With the Sharks Without Being Eaten Alive." In this well written and concise book, McKay stresses the importance of doing your homework and finding out all you can about your prospects and competitors, even going as far as finding out their hobbies, birthdays and favorite sports teams. Dale Carnegie wrote an enormous best seller called, "How to Win Friends and Influence People." In this book Mr. Carnegie wrote that everyone's favorite subject is themselves. The message that McKay and Carnegie teach and what Chuck Connors was obviously aware of, is that before you part your lips to tell others about yourself, probe to find out about them.

If you listen to a person, they will often tell you exactly what they require before doing business with you or what it is that they are looking for. Chuck Connors went to others and researched what Rickey was looking for. If you don't do your homework, then don't expect to pass the test. There is no glory in "winging it." And we all thought Chuck Connors acting career began in Westerns.

Action Points

1. What is important to those around you? Interests? Morals? Beliefs? Goals? Find out what is going on in the lives of others and what is important to them. This could be researching a customer before a sales call or a friend's interest before you purchase them a gift.

2. If you are in the business world do you know who your competitors are and what their marketing plan is?

3. Life is a series of presentations. It may be a presentation on the phone to ask someone out to dinner or a presentation to a group to purchase your product. Whatever it is, tailor your presentations and proposals to fit them. If you listen they will tell you what their needs are.

Quotes From Branch Rickey

"A great ballplayer is a player who will take a chance."

"Baseball people, and that includes myself, are slow to change and accept new ideas. I remember that it took years to persuade them to put numbers on uniforms."

"Cobb lived off the field as though he wished to live forever. He lived on the field as though it was his last day."

"Ethnic prejudice has no place in sports, and baseball must recognize that truth if it's to maintain stature as a national game."

"How to use your leisure time is the biggest problem of a ballplayer."

"I am alarmed at the subtle invasion of professional football, which is gaining preeminence over baseball. It's unthinkable."

I don't care if I was a ditch-digger at a dollar a day, I'd want to do my job better than the fellow next to me. I'd want to be the best at whatever I do."

"I don't like the subtle infiltration of 'something for nothing' philosophies into the very hearthstone of the American family. I believe that 'Thou shalt earn the bread by the sweat of thy face' was a benediction and not a penalty. Work is the zest of life; there is joy in its pursuit."

Quotes from Sandy Koufax

"A guy that throws what he intends to throw, that's the definition of a good pitcher."

"I became a good pitcher when I stopped trying to make them miss the ball and started trying to make them hit it."

"In the end it all comes down to talent. You can talk all you want about intangibles. I just don't know what that means. Talent makes winners, not intangibles. Can nice guys win? Sure, nice guys can win - if they're nice guys with a lot of talent. Nice guys with a little talent finish fourth and nice guys with no talent finish last."

"I think it's incredible because there were guys like Mays and Mantle and Henry Aaron who were great players for ten years... I only had four or five good years."

"People who write about spring training not being necessary have never tried to throw a baseball."

"Pitching is the art of instilling fear."

"Show me a guy who can't pitch inside and I'll show you a loser."

"The game has a cleanness. If you do a good job, the numbers say so. You don't have to ask anyone or play politics. You don't have to wait for the reviews."

LESSON NINE - "I WAS AS GOOD AS SANDY KOUFAX"

He was a Major League pitcher at the time. His record was 36-40 and he lacked control. The statistics of his first six seasons in the Major Leagues were average at best, and there was no reason to believe he would have a long professional career. Several years ago, I heard Nolan Ryan talk about him in an interview. That's right, a man that lost more games than he won in six seasons had the good fortune of his name crossing the lips of Hall-of-Famer, Nolan Ryan. What was this man's name? Sandy Koufax.

Sandy Koufax graced the Major Leagues for a total of 12 seasons. At least this is what the baseball almanac tells us. However, a strong argument could be made that Koufax had two careers in the Majors--one career from 1955 to 1960 and another from 1961 to 1966. The second Sandy Koufax is most likely the one that you have heard of and the one that etched his place into the minds and hearts of baseball fans-- the one with dominating pitches, three Cy Young awards, five ERA titles, and the 1963 MVP.

Nolan Ryan said in an interview, "At times, I believe I was as good as Sandy Koufax." Nolan, that is without a doubt true and although you were unsurprisingly modest when you said it, it was an extremely bold statement. It was bold because Sandy Koufax was one of the most dominating men ever to stand sixty feet six inches from home plate with a baseball in his mitt. In his final season, he chalked 27 wins on the board for the Dodgers and posted a remarkable 1.73 ERA.

For the first six years of his career there was no evidence in the game log that the last six would be any different. What made the difference? Any one thing probably can't be singled out as the difference maker. But, with that said, a significant event occurred in 1961 that shaped the future of Sandy

Koufax. The event came in the form of a suggestion generated from a man who did not make the Hall-of-Fame. He was a man who played only five seasons in the Major Leagues. This ballplayer ended his career as a lifetime .215 hitter and his last season he batted only .136 in 147 at-bats. However, Koufax was willing to listen to advice.

The man who generously submitted his thoughts was a catcher who had watched Koufax throw. After observing Koufax, the catcher noticed that he was putting too much force behind each pitch. He suggested Koufax ease up and throw more change-ups and curves.

Who did this man think he was? The name on the back of his jersey was Sherry and his first name was Norm. Sherry was a reserve catcher. If he knew anything about pitching, he would be a pitcher...well, that isn't what Koufax thought. He took Sherry's advice and won 18 games that season, the most in his career and more than the combined total of the two previous seasons. Oddly enough, Koufax led the league with 269 strikeouts that year by "easing up" on his pitches.

We can learn a lot from observing the career of Sandy Koufax. But, there are two lessons that really stand out. First, accept constructive criticism regardless of who it comes from. Second, you can "try" too hard.

It would have been very easy for Sandy Koufax to ignore the advice of a man who had failed to make his mark on professional baseball. It would have been easy for Koufax to think, "Who is this man?" It would have been easy. However, he didn't do that. A person who can't accept constructive criticism is most often fighting to convince the individual giving the advice that they are off base. Koufax did not invest one minute in that worthless use of time. He listened and got better.

I have a very successful friend who instructed his employees to list his faults and blind spots and present them. Each employee prepared a list and at one o'clock the next day took their places in the meeting room. My friend sat at the head of the table with a pen and paper and began the meeting by thanking everyone for the time they had invested in this effort and then asked them to go around the room and list what they had written down. Most only had one or two points. One employee listed 23 items or ways that my friend could improve! That was a humbling day. Yet, he sat there and didn't make a sound, only nodding and writing each point down.

Who were these people? Their income was a fraction of his. Most likely they will never obtain the success in business that he had. Yet, he humbled himself and asked others what he was doing wrong. Most spend their days toiling to show everyone what they are doing right. He went out of his way to ask others what he was doing wrong. Sandy Koufax did the same and has a Hall-of-Fame ring to show for it.

You can learn something from every single person in your life. It's obvious that you can learn from the successful people. It's not so obvious that you can learn from everyone. Treat everyone's opinion the same. Show no favoritism, humble yourself and never give up in your effort to be better.

And Nolan, yes you were as good as Koufax.

Action Points

1. Has someone suggested an improvement that you scoffed at because you didn't respect what he or she had accomplished?

2. Are you open to other's suggestions?

3. Do you spend so much time trying to convince others that you have it all together that you wouldn't even hear constructive criticism?

4. Are you willing to be a Norm Sherry? A person who tactfully offers advice to see others improve?

5. Are you willing to ask others for advice?

"I knew it would ruin my arm, but one year of 25-7 is worth five of 15- 15."
Steve Stone

"If I had my career to play over, one thing I'd do differently is swing more. Those 1,200 walks I got, nobody remembers them."
Pee Wee Reese

"Baseball players are smarter than football players. How often do you see a baseball team penalized for too many men on the field?"
Jim Bouton

"...You say Mickey Mantle, I'll say Willie Mays; if you say Henry Aaron, I'll say Roberto Clemente. When you're comparing at that level of ability, the margins of difference aren't that great."
Tom Seaver

"My motto was to always keep swinging. Whether I was in a slump or feeling badly or having trouble off the field, the only thing to do was keep swinging."
Hank Aaron

"The difference between impossible and possible lies within a man's determination."
-Tommy LaSorda

LESSON TEN – SOUTHPAWS

Sandy Koufax, Babe Ruth, Lefty Grove, Steve Carlton, Randy Johnson and Warren Spahn are some of baseball's all-time best pitchers. They also share one common trait. They are all left handed or "southpaws." Most Major League pitchers (about 70%) are right handed. This stands to reason because most of the general population tends to be right handed. But, why in the world would you call a left handed pitcher a "southpaw?"

We can find the answer in the way ballparks traditionally have been constructed. Stadium architects will do everything they can in advance to prohibit any obstruction to the "batter's eye." In straight away centerfield, just over the wall of most ballparks, you'll find an area where there is a break in the stands. No one is allowed to sit or stand in this area. This area is typically grass or some other solid dark color. By doing this, chances are less likely that a batter will "lose" the ball in a light background or a fan's clothing. In the 2001 World Series Yankees third baseman Scott Brosius, "lost" the ball on a grounder to third in a banner that was hanging on the wall between the field and the stands. The banner was promptly removed. The league will go out of its way to assure that an outside force doesn't affect anything that occurs on the field.

In addition, the league has given thought to the certainty of nature. One of the laws of nature is that the sun will rise in the east and set in the west. This is a universal truth. Therefore, home plate is typically at the west-end of the field with second base being to the east placing batters so that they would face away from the sunset and there would be no chance of losing the ball in the glare.

If second base faces the east, then first base must be at the south end of the field. A left-handed pitcher, when standing on the mound has his pitching arm to the first base side of the infield. The first base side of the infield is the south side. Consequently, a left-handed pitcher is often referred to as a "southpaw."

Think about that for a minute. In the construction of a ballpark, the direction that home plate will face is considered before a grain of sand is moved. It's a given fact that there will be no one sitting in straight away centerfield to distract the batter. Major League Baseball has put a lot of advance work in planning baseball fields and avoiding problems.

I am reminded of a story of a young salesman for a kitchenware company. One day he realized how he was spending all of his time crisscrossing town and little time giving sales presentations. He asked himself how he could overcome this problem. He decided that every night he would map out his sales calls. He scheduled all of his morning calls in a certain area of town and then his afternoon calls would be conducted on the other side of town. This enabled him to see twice as many prospects every week!

The salesman's closing ratio didn't change one percentage point. The only thing that changed was his planning. He doubled his income by simply planning in advance. Baseball has done this by deciding in advance what things could keep a batter from peak performance and then has eliminated them from the batter's equation for success.

There you have it. "Southpaw" is a name given to left-handed pitchers because their left hand faces the south end of the field. The reason that their left hand faces south is because baseball believes planning and strategy are ingredients to success. They're right. Let's use that knowledge in our life.

Action Points

1. Without considering the solutions list the common problems of your daily life?

2. Now, what are some possible solutions to these problems?

3. Do you plan your work and then work your plan?

4. Do you utilize a day timer or organizer?

"You start chasing a ball and your brain immediately commands your body to run forward! Bend! Scoop up the ball! Peg it to first! Then your body says who me?"
Joe DiMaggio

"I am throwing twice as hard as I ever did. It is just not getting there as fast."
Lefty Gomez

"We used to go to the racetrack after spring training practice in my day. Four of us would chip in fifty cents each to go to the two-dollar window. Yesterday, I asked a player how he did at the track. He said 'my horse won.' I said, 'how much did it pay?' The player said, 'no, coach, I didn't bet on the horse, I own it.'"
Yankee Coach Mickey Vernon, 1985

"Fans don't boo nobodies."
Reggie Jackson

"The guy with the biggest stomach will be the first to take off his shirt at a baseball game."
Glenn Dickey

LESSON ELEVEN - ONE THING IN COMMON

Willie Mays, Lou Gehrig, Mickey Mantle, Kirk Gibson, Nolan Ryan, Ozzie Smith, Pete Rose, Mike Schmidt, Buddy Bell, Goose Gossage, "Oil Can" Boyd, "Dizzy" Dean and Jackie Robinson. These are all phenomenal baseball players. They also have one thing in common. There is one thing that is true about every single one of them. There are probably many things, but will you think of this one?

One of the common threads these men possess is that their baseball careers are over and for many of them their lives are over. Each of these men is mortal. Each of these men reached a time in their career when they could no longer compete at a high level because their bodies began to rebel against the work regiment and challenges. Some could no longer throw a ball fast enough to zoom past Major League hitters who seemed to be getting younger and younger. Many found themselves swinging too late all too often at pitches they once could hit with ease. Their eyes refused to give them a clear picture of where the ball was going and their legs appeared asleep as they scampered to beat out a slow grounder.

I would give anything to watch Sandy Koufax pitch against Barry Bonds or Nolan Ryan strike out Babe Ruth. However, I will never see that. The reason I won't is that every man, woman and child lives their lives on a chronological timeline of birth, growth, climax and decay. Some lives are cut short before the cycle naturally occurs. However, what is certain is that the cycle will occur. The statistic is one out of one will experience the cycle of life and death. In a game of numbers and statistics, that is one statistic that has not wavered in thousands of years.

Ted Williams was asked in the late '90's, "If you were playing today against current pitchers, what do you think you would bat?" Mr. Williams replied, "Oh...about .200" The interviewer was stunned. "Mr. Williams, you mean that you, in your prime, would only bat .200 against today's pitchers?" He replied, "Oh, I'm sorry. I thought that you meant if I was playing today at my current age!" That story should illustrate Ted Williams didn't lack confidence even in his seventies!

I wish I could see Ted Williams bat today, but I can't. You see the time line of my life did not overlap with the playing time of Ted Williams, Sandy Koufax, Jackie Robinson or Babe Ruth. Friend, life is precious. These men will never get the chance to play professional base ball again. Many have passed on. They will never again know the excitement of the crowd or the thrill in hearing their bat crack. Their time has come and the sun has set on their careers. Now, they must hope that the work they put in will stand the test of time.

Even Lou Gehrig's and Cal Ripken's "Iron Man" streaks came to an end because of the cycle of life. If there were two men who have ever made a case that it doesn't have to end, that they are immortal and will play forever, it's these two spectacular men. But, Gehrig's streak was ended by a disease that shortly thereafter took his life and Ripken's streak ended because the natural cycle of life had taken its toll on the body of a man who was ready to exit the game. I wish it didn't have to end, however, it does. If for just a moment you think you may be an exception, look at Gehrig and Ripken. If they are vulnerable, how can we outrun the cycle of life and death that is chasing each one of us?

Every day each of us has 86,400 seconds to use and spend wisely. Once the time is gone, it's gone. The statistics have not changed since the dawn of time--one out of one people will have a dawn and sunset to their life. Even the players like Babe Ruth who seemed immortal and larger than life were mortal. The day did come when he could no longer perform his baseball tasks at a high level. No one is immortal. No one is larger than life and eventually, the ninth inning will come for each of us. Whether we win or lose is determined by what we do in those nine innings.

Your time will come, just like it did for the Babe, Lou Gehrig, Nolan Ryan and every other player who set foot on the baseball diamond. One day your flesh and bones will be spent. Make the most of every time at bat and every game. Give it your best every day and when you are done, hope your life shows that you did.

Play fast, play the game right, work hard, touch all the bases, and have fun, because one day, you won't be able to.

ACTION POINTS

1. Realize that you are mortal.

2. You have a limited amount of time in life. What percentage are you spending with family versus working?

3. How can you benefit more from the way you spend your time?

4. When you are working, how can you maximize your time?

"The way a team plays as a whole determines its success. You may have the greatest bunch of individual stars in the world, but if they don't play together, the club won't be worth a dime."
Babe Ruth

"Good pitching will always stop good hitting and vice-versa."
Casey Stengel

"Somebody will hit .400 again. Somebody will get smart and swing naturally."
Ty Cobb

"Above anything else, I hate to lose."
Jackie Robinson

"Ain't no man can avoid being born average, but there ain't no man got to be common."
Satchel Paige

"The team that wins two-thirds of its one-run games usually wins the pennant."
Pete Rose

"Do they leave it there during the game?"
Bill Lee after first seeing Fenway's Green Monster

"Anybody with ability can play in the big leagues. But to be able to trick people year in and year out the way I did, I think that was a much greater feat."
Bob Uecker

LESSON TWELVE - SAY HEY

The Giants had a 2-1 lead over the Dodgers in the eighth inning of a highly intense battle. The Dodgers were batting with one out and runners on the corners. Carl Furillo nails what is sure to be an RBI ball and possibly a base hit to right center. The outfielder dashes to the ball, with his hat flying off, and back to the plate he makes an over-the-shoulder catch in deep right center. He immediately stops dead in his tracks, pivots and throws a laser beam to home plate. He threw the runner out from third that was five feet from scoring! The crowd was silent for a brief, stunned moment. No one could believe what they'd just seen. Then they erupted in overwhelming jubilation. They had just witnessed a most improbable double play.

You may have guessed who the outfielder was. The clues are: over the shoulder, hat flying off and Giants outfield. Who else could it be but "The Say Hey Kid," Willie Mays? There have been very few ball players like Willie Mays. He played 22 seasons and concluded with a .303 batting average. He is third all time in home runs, sixth in runs scored, and led the league for three consecutive years in stolen bases.

Willie Mays was not only an incredible athlete with superb talents that through discipline and hard work he perfected, he was also a master showman and illusionist. In 1991, the 60-year-old Willie let the baseball world in on a little secret. Baseball writers used to love to write about the way that Willie's hat would fly off as he rounded the diamond. As he sprinted the 90 feet between the bases his hat would typically fly off. After he reached base safely, he would call time out and slowly walk back to pick up his hat. The fans loved it. They would exclaim, "His hat flew off he was running so fast!" Not exactly...

Willie revealed, at the age of 60, that it wasn't so amazing that his hat would fly off. You see...Willie intentionally wore a hat that was too large for his head. He purposefully tilted his head when he ran so that the oversized hat would fly off. This added to the legend of his speed. Was he fast? You betcha. He led the league three straight years in stolen bases. But, Willie also understood something very important about sizzle and impressions. He understood that his hat flying off excited everyone and made him appear even faster than he was. Willie was a master showman and created quite a stir with this little detail that he added to spice up the game.

I personally am not a flashy guy. I don't wear a watch or any jewelry. You will never see me with a necklace or bracelet of any kind. However, when I speak before a group or enter a business meeting you will never find me in anything but the nicest suit and freshly ironed shirt. I watch every detail.

As a young speaker in Houston, I was pulled aside after giving a speech to a telecommunications company. (I began public speaking at the age of 20 and had a lot to learn.) The owner of the company sat me down and picked apart my speech. He told me how defensive I was in handling objections. He pointed to my unpolished shoes and wrinkled shirt and told me that because of those things, he would never do business with me. At the time, I was insulted. Today, I am grateful.

Willie also showed us the importance of sizzle and impressions. I find ways in my speeches to be a showman and amaze the crowd a little. I will often get everyone's name in the audience (even if there are 100 people in the room) and then when I leave, call everyone by name! I use a memory technique that I learned a long time ago, and with that showmanship make a permanent impression on the group.

All too often we shrug aside the importance of impressions and forget that people are always watching. Someone is always watching no matter what you are doing. Everything you do matters, even the little things. When we are well groomed, well dressed, physically fit and well rested people notice. If those things are in place they will add to the overall impression. Appearance does count. Outward appearance does matter. With a little sizzle people will remember you forever. Be flashy. Even if it's not in the way you dress. Find a way to add some sizzle to your presentations. Willie did...Say Hey.

ACTION POINTS

1. Is your appearance as good as it can be?

2. What kind of first impression do you make?

3. Do you look others in the eye and listen to them?

4. What do you do to separate yourself from the pack?

5. How can you add sizzle in your business life? How can you spice things up?

LESSON THIRTEEN - I'M GONNA HIT IT OUT!

It was October 1932 and the New York Yankees were playing the Chicago Cubs in the World Series. To this day it is hotly contested whether Ruth did, in fact, call his shot. By way of background, the event occurred in the third game of an intense series. The Yankees had won the first two games and the Cubs seemed to be venting their frustrations on the 37 year old Ruth, who was nearing the end of his career.

It was the top of the fifth inning, and the score was deadlocked at 4-4. Ruth was being taunted, not only by the boisterous fans, but jeers were also coming from the Cub dugout. He was called fat and over the hill. Charlie Root, the Cub pitcher, quickly secured a two-strike count on Ruth. Legend has it that this is when Ruth held his lumber in his hand and pointed it to centerfield, signaling to Root and his teammates exactly where he intended to plant the next pitch-- quite a confident gesture to say the least. If he had missed, we wouldn't still be talking about that day 75 years later. But he didn't miss.

Have you ever thought about how hard it is to hit a Major League pitch? The average pitch is 88 miles per hour. The distance from the pitchers mound to home plate is sixty feet six inches. But, the pitcher takes a stride when he throws and actually throws it approximately fifty-five feet. This gives the batter about four tenths of a second before the pitch reaches home plate. However, the batter can not wait until the pitch arrives to react. He must judge the pitch almost immediately. This gives the batter about only three tenths of a second to react!

Not only did Babe Ruth react in three tenths of a second to clobber a home run to centerfield, he predicted it! Sports writer Rich Vidmer described the called shot by saying, "Before Ruth left the plate and started his swing around the bases, he paused to laugh at the Chicago players, suddenly silent in their dugout. As he rounded, he flung a remark at Grimm, as he turned second he tossed a jest at Billy Herman, and his shoulders shook with satisfaction as he trotted."

What did Babe Ruth do? He said what he was going to do and then he did it. All the while he humorously, to many, gloated about it. I certainly can say that he had the right to gloat. All too often in life, many will not do what they say they are going to do. Yet worse, most will not even say what they are going to do. The human mind is an incredibly powerful tool that if used properly can be your servant. When you visualize your goals and even declare them, you are programming your mind for success.

Napoleon Hill was the author of a ground breaking book called, "Think and Grow Rich." The theme of this book was the value of autosuggestion, exactly the technique Babe Ruth, perhaps unknowingly, employed. By consciously visualizing our goals and then publicly stating them, we are actually programming ourselves for success.

Mr. Ruth, it has been debated whether you actually called this shot. But, what can't be debated is your legend and abilities. Thank you for the memories and this lesson on goal setting.

ACTION POINTS

1. Do you have clearly defined goals?

2. Write down your business goals for the next year:

3. Write down your personal goals for the next year:

4. Create timelines and deadlines for the accomplishment of these goals.

5. Be careful of the images you allow your mind to create and dwell upon. Bad programming is worse than no programming.

"The most important things in life are good friends and a strong bullpen."
Bob Lemon

"If a tie is like kissing your sister, losing is like kissing your grandmother with her teeth out."
George Brett

"Baseball is like church. Many attend but few understand."
Wes Westrum

More quotes from Yogi Berra
"Why buy good luggage? You only use it when you travel."

"When you come to a fork in the road take it."

"We're lost but we're making good time."

"If the world were perfect it wouldn't be."

"If I didn't wake up I'd still be sleeping."

"I usually take a two hour nap from 1 to 4."

"If you can't imitate him, don't copy him."

"It gets late early out here."

"90% of the game is half mental."

"Always go to other people's funerals otherwise they won't go to yours."

"Steve McQueen looks good in this movie. He must have made it before he died."

"I'm as red as a sheet."

"Pair up in threes."

Lesson Fourteen –
Cooperstown

Abner Doubleday is said to be the inventor of baseball. It turns out this is just a nice legend with no basis in truth. However, Abner's hometown of Cooperstown, New York is home to the Baseball Hall of Fame anyway. Every year retired baseball hopefuls eagerly wait to see if they will receive baseball's highest honor, to be selected as the elite cream of the crop. It's the crowning touch on an incredible career.

Induction into the Hall of Fame is not the only award that professional baseball offers its players. Think about it for a minute. As players press on through their 162 games, and hopefully more, there is the MVP, the Cy Young Award, the All-Star game, Rookie of the Year, Comeback Player of the Year, Batting Champion, Gold Glove, and many others. Why do Major League players need awards? Why does a man making $10 million a year need a plaque to hang on his wall? Why is being inducted into the Hall of Fame often accompanied with tears and the signing of a $100 million contract accompanied by a smile?

The answer is simple. It's because the ballplayers who play this game are human. That's right it's because they are people just like you and me. You see, people need recognition and respect, especially men. It's a driving motivation or force. The thought of making $250 million in ten years is also a powerful driving force, but the reason a plaque that weighs five pounds also packs such a powerful punch is because it stands for recognition and appreciation. Everyone needs to know they are appreciated and that their work was noticed. How many people do you know who are feeling discouraged? All it might take to bring a smile to their face or tear to their eye is a simple word of acknowledgment or appreciation. We all need it, even if you are making $10 million per year.

Baseball is a game of recognition and statistics. There are more numbers in baseball than in any other game. You have ERA's, RBI's, on-base percentage, slugging percentage, walks per nine innings, batting average, batting average against left handed pitching, batting average against right handed pitching, stolen bases, strikeouts, home runs and the list goes on. There are several reasons for the statistics. They allow managers to plan their strategy with educated moves, and they also allow the ballplayer to gauge his performance and measure his talents.

Baseball can teach us two very important lessons here if we let it. The first lesson would be that people thrive on rewards and awards. Whether you're making $25,000 per year or $25,000 per game, recognition and awards motivate and drive you. Do not let anyone around you have their good efforts go unrecognized. The second lesson is to track your success.

Can you imagine not knowing how many home runs Babe Ruth belted? Or how many batters Nolan Ryan struck out? As crazy as it sounds, many sales professionals don't know how many sales they have closed this week, month or year. Many don't track their personal progress in any fashion. While rewards are important, they are impossible without tracking results.

Recognize and reward your successes as well as the success of those around you, and I will see you at the Cooperstown of life.

Action Points

1. If you have numbers in your business that are important, do you track them?

2. If so, how?

3. Do you openly recognize your successes and the successes of others?

4. What awards are established for your organization?

5. What awards could you establish?

6. Make it known what the criteria for the awards are.

7. Make sure every department has its own special award.

8. Become diligent at tracking your numbers

Quotes from Ernie Banks

"Did you hear that? I didn't hear anything. Put that question another way."

"I like my players to be married and in debt. That's the way you motivate them."

"It's a great day for a ballgame; let's play two!"

"The Cubs are due in sixty-two."

"The Cubs are gonna' shine in sixty-nine."

"The only way to prove that you're a good sport is to lose."

"The riches of the game are in the thrills, not the money."

"You must try to generate happiness within yourself. If you aren't happy in one place, chances are you won't be happy anyplace."

LESSON FIFTEEN - THREE OUNCES

If you took a poll of all Major League baseball players and asked them, "What position did you play in the little leagues?" I think that you'd find "shortstop" to be the number one response. The reason I think that is simple; the position of shortstop requires perhaps the most athletic ability of any position in baseball. Speed, agility and arm strength are all factors in deciding who will play shortstop. There is no doubt that the men playing in the Major Leagues today, 20 years ago were the most athletic of their little league team.

Shortstop requires so much athletic ability that many teams are willing to give up power numbers or a high batting average to get someone who will consistently stop balls and make the plays. A good shortstop can take runs off the opposition's score by playing great defense. Ozzie Smith, who played 19 years with the Padres and Cardinals hit only 28 home runs in his entire career, and had a lifetime .262 batting average. He played 19 years because of his glove, not his bat.

There have been shortstops in baseball history who've possessed both the bat and the glove. Before Alex Rodriguez and Derek Jeter, there was Ernie Banks. He led the league in 1958 with 47 home runs and in 1960 with 41 round trippers. In 1958 and 1959 he led the league in RBI's.

Banks wasn't a slouch in the field either. He made as many outstanding plays with his glove as he did with a bat and was a rare commodity at shortstop because of it. In 1959 he hit 45 home runs, drove in 143, batted .304 and made only 12 errors all season. That phenomenal year earned him the National League's MVP Award.

Many baseball players have what is called a breakthrough year, a year where they break some invisible barrier and perform at an all-star level. For Ernie Banks that was 1954. That year he clobbered 44 home runs. However, the year before he had only cranked 19 homers out of the yard. What made the difference? A lot of things made the difference, but straight from the mouth of the man himself "it was the bat." The year before he swung a 34-ounce bat and recalled that it began to feel like "a telephone pole." He made the switch to a 31-ounce model and it "felt like I was swishing a broomstick."

This went against the wisdom of the day. It was believed that the heavier the bat the farther the ball went. The weight of the bat was believed to help the ball over the fence. Later it was realized that bat speed combined with the weight of the bat propelled the ball over the fence, and a lighter bat might mean more bat speed. In 1949 only 14 percent of the bats used in the Major Leagues weighed 32 ounces or less. By 1959 the number had increased to nearly 70 percent.

Success fans the fire of imitation, and soon ball players around the league were trading in their heavy bats for a lighter piece of wood. Banks had found success with his new bat, however think about it for a minute. Three ounces. That's it! Three ounces. How much weight could that be? The answer is not much, but a lot.

You see, in life, the difference between success and failure is not a giant canyon. Instead, it's a small crack that many never cross. The difference between the man living on the street and the man who owns the largest building on the street are little characteristics--qualities of simply being faithful, punctual and hard working. They are qualities that we can all exemplify and in reality few of us do. What's the difference between success and failure? Well, just lighten the bat. The difference is very little and yet, a lot. A little because of the fact that we are already most likely doing many of the things that will lead to success, and a lot because discovering what the little things are requires work and mental toughness. Those small things can be a lot.

The difference of 19 home runs and 44 home runs in one season was in part due to 3 ounces. Don't miss your success by three ounces. Remember the lesson that Banks taught us. In every endeavor the difference between success and failure is often not a giant canyon, but a small crack. In many cases the small crack can be overtaken with only minor tweaking to what you are already doing.

ACTION POINTS

1. Remember that success is often the results of minor tweaking and not a major overhaul.

2. Remember that the difference between the most successful person in the world and the pauper is often nothing more than the results of small daily choices.

3. You are probably closer to magnificent success than you realize.

4. In what area of your life do you need a breakthrough?

5. Is there any piece of this area that you could change just a little?

"A life is not important except in the impact it has on other lives."

Jackie Robinson

Lesson Sixteen — Others

Johnny Oates is a man and a baseball figure, but first and foremost, a man of the highest caliber. Mr. Oates is the definition of what a man, father, husband, grandfather, coach and leader should be. Some may not be aware of Johnny Oates. His career as a baseball player and coach lasted thirty-four years. He played for Atlanta, Philadelphia, Baltimore, New York and Los Angeles in a total of 593 games. He was a lifetime .250 hitter with 14 home runs and 126 RBI's. He managed three Minor League teams and then managed the Baltimore Orioles and the Texas Rangers.

Oates shared Manager of the Year honors with Joe Torre in 1996. He led the Rangers to division titles in '96, '98 and '99. Oates was respected by his players and was well liked everywhere he went. He had a very good baseball career, but that isn't why I remember Johnny Oates. One of the reasons I remember him is because of something that happened in his first year with Texas. Just before the season began, Oates' wife, Gloria, became ill. He left the team to be with her. This was his first year with the team and everyone wants to make a good impression when they have just begun a new job, but Oates turned the reigns over to his assistant coach during the first few weeks of the season and went home to be with his wife.

Oates made no apologies for placing his wife and family above his career. I remember reading the sports page and admiring the man for his decision. In his final year with the Texas Rangers, I watched the man break down and cry in a television press conference. He had been corresponding for a year and a half with a young boy who had leukemia. This man, who was managing a Major League baseball team and had a demanding schedule, found time to write letters to a young boy who could offer him nothing. This boy could give him nothing in return but friendship and an occasional letter. However, for Oates that was enough.

Before the press conference Oates had received a letter from his father saying that the boy had passed away. I watched him fight back tears and choke up as he talked about the boy and said, "Life is a lot more than just wins and losses." A boy who died had touched the heart of an extremely powerful man. It touched a heart of a man who put others first and genuinely cared about
people.

When I watched Johnny during that press conference, I was surprised by the man's caring words. Although at this point, I don't know why I was surprised because I should have been used to it from him.

Oates had health problems of his own just a short time later. He was diagnosed with a Gliobastoma Multiforme tumor, the most aggressive type of brain tumor. Doctors told Oates that one year is the average life expectancy after being diagnosed with this type of tumor. Although he surpassed the one year life expectancy, he passed away in December of 2004 as a result of the tumor.

In an interview with a local Texas newspaper when talking about his illness, Oates said, "Assure everyone that I am at peace right now." That really struck me; at a time like this, he wanted to put the mind of others at ease. Think about that for a minute. In his serious, serious condition, he wanted to put everyone else at ease. That is the definition of a man – someone who thinks of the interests of others before the interests of himself.

Oates was an average player, a very good manager and one heck of a human being. Oates put others before himself. Oates was a servant. He realized the importance of people.

Whether it was sitting by his wife's bed, writing to a young boy or easing the minds of his fans when he was facing death, he knew how to care about others.

Although it sounds simple, it really isn't. If it was simple, everyone would do it and I wouldn't get goose bumps when I read that Oates wanted "everyone to be at ease" when he was the one facing the illness. That was Johnny Oates, a model of what it means to put others first.

The success lesson from the remarkable life of Johnny Oates is obvious--that whether it is personal or professional, if we approach others with the attitude of what we can give to the transaction or relationship or
put another way--what we can do for others--then we are going to have much more success than if we seek every encounter as an opportunity to add to our literal or emotional bank account.

It has been said that you can tell a lot about a person by the way they treat those who can do nothing for them. If that's true, and I believe it is, Johnny Oates was one heck of a man.

ACTION POINTS

1. What do you do on a daily basis to show your family that you care about them?

2. What do you do on a regular basis to demonstrate to your coworkers or family that they are appreciated?

3. How do you treat those who can do nothing for you?

4. In your decision making processes, whose best interest do you think of? It isn't wrong to think of your best interest, however do you consider others?

5. Is there something simple that you could do to show interest in others such as corresponding via mail or email, making a weekly phone call or having dinner with someone? Find someone who can do nothing in return for you. Find someone who has nothing to offer you but time and friendship. Johnny Oates did.

"I can sit in a ballpark after a game and love looking at the field. Everybody's gone, and the ballpark is empty, and I'll sit there. I sit there and think, 'Is this as close to heaven as I'm going to get?' Or, 'If I get to heaven, will there be baseball?'"
Kim Braatz-Voisard, Silver Bullets' center fielder, 1997

"It is designed to break your heart. The game begins in the spring, when everything else begins again, and it blossoms in the summer, filling the afternoons and evenings, and then as soon as the chill rains come, it stops and leaves you to face the fall alone."
A. Bartlett Giamatti, "The Green Fields of the Mind"

"Let us go forth awhile, and get better air in our lungs. Let us leave our closed rooms... The game of ball is glorious."
Walt Whitman

"Holy Cow!"
Harry Carey

"Now, you tell me, if I have a day off during the baseball season, where do you think I'll spend it? The ballpark. I still love it; always have, always will."
Harry Carey, on his reason not to retire

"Hitting is 50% above the shoulders."
Ted Williams

"Hitting is timing. Pitching is upsetting timing."
Warren Spahn

"Career highlights? I had two. I got an intentional walk from Sandy Koufax and I got out of a rundown against the Mets."
Bob Uecker

"I would like to take the great DiMaggio fishing, the old man said. They say his father was a fisherman. Maybe he was as poor as we are and would understand."
Ernest Hemingway in The Old Man and the Sea

"Best one-legged player I ever saw."
Casey Stengle on the often injured Mickey Mantle

"The one constant through all the years, Ray, has been baseball. America has rolled by like an army of steamrollers. It's been erased like a blackboard, rebuilt, and erased again. But baseball has marked the time. This field, this game, is a part of our past, Ray. It reminds us of all that once was good, and that could be again. Oh people will come, Ray. People will most definitely come."
James Earl Jones as Terence Mann, in Field of Dreams

"You look forward to it like a party when you're a kid. You think something wonderful is going to happen."
Joe DiMaggio regarding opening day

LESSON SEVENTEEN - OPENING DAY

The official signal that spring has landed is the hoisting of stars and stripes, the scent of freshly manicured grass, organ music being played in cities around the country and the crack of a bat. More than 40,000 bodies become one face as they move in unison to their feet to cheer a 95-mile per hour fastball or a 400-foot home run. On this day everyone owns first place. There is no talk of magic numbers, disappointing seasons, pennant races or who will be back next year.

President George W. Bush writes in his book, A Charge to Keep:

"This is our year that optimism says every year, opening day of the baseball season, we win the pennant. No matter that the same scene is replayed in every Major League ballpark in America, on every opening day, it always seems entirely possible, imminently doable that this year, it's our dream, our team, our pennant. In this way baseball is like every other major endeavor of my life. Baseball is a pursuit for optimists, just like drilling for oil or running for office. To come to the ballpark every day you have to believe that you can win. To drill another well after a dry hole, you have to believe that this one will succeed."

President George W. Bush is a man who knows baseball and a man who knows trials and success. He is right--baseball is about optimism. Opening day celebrates every team's dream that this is the year.

Without that dream and possibility, opening day would lose its magic for everyone. I love watching teams go from worst to first. They forget about last season and start again with a fresh new perspective. It's true that teams like the Yankees have a distinct financial advantage. However, it is also true that regular teams like the Oakland Athletics and smaller market teams are competing and winning without the largest payrolls.

Opening day is a day for optimists. It's a day that celebrates the birth of the yearly contest. At this single moment in time, every team possesses first place and is equidistant from the prize of the World Series. In 2002, I watched the Minnesota Twins, with one of the lowest payrolls in baseball, in the midst of a thick pennant race with the Cleveland Indians. The Twins began spring training with a youthful team and very low payroll. Yet, they carried the optimism and fire from spring training and opening day into the regular season and almost pulled off a most improbable pennant. The Twins proved that any team can compete. Don't miss the next opening day. It's a day for celebration and optimism.

How about you? Have you lost that optimism? Have you drilled one too many holes only to find it dry? Have you forgotten to start over with a fresh perspective? Have you forgotten that this year someone will win and that it could be you? Have you forgotten that many teams go from worst to first?

ACTION POINTS

1. Remember that you can start over. List an area of your life where you could use a fresh start.

2. Remain optimistic. What can you do to start fresh?

3. A worst place finish last year doesn't mean a last place finish this year. What do you currently do to celebrate new beginnings?

4. What could you do?

Quotes by Ted Williams

"A man has to have goals - for a day, for a lifetime - and that was mine, to have people say, 'There goes Ted Williams, the greatest hitter who ever lived.'"

"Baseball gives every American boy a chance to excel, not just to be as good as someone else but to be better than someone else. This is the nature of man and the name of the game."

"Baseball is the only field of endeavor where a man can succeed three times out of ten and be considered a good performer."

"Baseball's future? Bigger and bigger, better and better! No question about it, it's the greatest game there is!"

"By the time you know what to do, you're too old to do it."

"DiMaggio was the greatest all-around player I ever saw. His career cannot be summed up in numbers and awards. It might sound corny, but he had a profound and lasting impact on the country."

"Hitting is the most important part of the game. It is where the big money is, where much of the status is, and the fan interest."

"If I was being paid thirty-thousand dollars a year, the very least I could do was hit .400."

Lesson Eighteen – Control

Steve Dalkowski is a man who will forever be remembered as one of the greatest power pitchers of all time. Major League batters for years marveled at how his pitches seemed to travel 110 miles per hour.

Dalkowski has taken his place in the Baseball Hall of Fame. What's that? You have never heard of the man who regularly threw over 100 miles per hour? Well, don't feel alone. Not many fans have ever heard of Steve Dalkowski. Yet, he may have been the pitcher who possessed the most powerful fastball of all time.

Steve only had one problem--his control. He spent time in the Minor Leagues from 1957 to 1965, but never made it to the big leagues for one reason. That's right--control. Players could not hit his fastball. He pitched 1,000 innings in the minors and struck out 1,400 batters. That is pretty amazing. Unfortunately for Dalkowski, he also walked as many batters as he struck out and had a life time ERA of 5.59. He lost twice as many games as he won and quit baseball at the age of twenty-six.

How could a man with so much natural talent be so unsuccessful? The answer, once again for those not listening, is control. How many times have we seen a young player with so much potential not live up to expectations? How many times have we seen the spotlight, money and fame sidetrack a promising athlete? Now, this is not the kind of problem Steve Dalkowski had. His control problem was that he physically could not control the baseball enough to keep it in the strike zone. However, think about other young players who did not make their mark because of money, fame or the spotlight. What failed them? Their control failed them, their ability to say no to the things that would derail them. The lure of sex, money, power, laziness, and complacency captured their minds. They could not harness their abilities and their mind.

Our thirtieth President, Calvin Coolidge said:
"Nothing in this world can take the place of persistence. Talent will not; nothing is more common than unsuccessful men with talent; genius will not; un-rewarded genius is almost a proverb. Education will not; the world is full of educated derelicts. Persistence and determination alone are omnipotent."

In those words, President Coolidge explained that there is nothing more common than unsuccessful men with talent. I can't think of many things worse than possessing everything you need to cross the finish line and not crossing that finish line because of a self imposed barrier of lack of control in any area. More often than not, issues of control are mental matters.

The star second baseman for the Minnesota Twins and New York Yankees, Chuck Knoblauch, demonstrated what a mental barrier can do to a person. Knoblauch was a ball player who performed masterfully at second base for years and then one day found himself unable to throw the ball accurately to first base. His manager, Joe Torre, tried everything from sports psychiatrists to throwing drills, but nothing seemed to help. A mental obstacle had formed in Knoblauch's mind, and he no longer possessed control. Eventually, he was moved to right field because his mental block was hurting the team.

Overcoming lack of control, whether it be mental, sexual, lust for money, power or complacency is a challenge for the greatest minds. Combating lack of control can take someone their entire life. The human mind is more powerful than the greatest computer ever created. It can store more data, process more calculations and plan for the future better than any CPU ever created.

In combating control, use the power of your CPU. The answer lies in your mind. Refuse to see yourself failing. Refuse to visualize yourself falling short of a mark. Focus only on success and refuse to accept failure as an option. If you are a pitcher, consult the expert pitching coaches on what the perfect mechanics look like. Then practice those mechanics until they resonate off the corners of your mind like words to your favorite song. You can use this same strategy for success if you are a pilot, speaker, sales professional or corporate executive. Do not discount the power of consulting experts. Many control issues find their root in the frailty of the human condition. The expert in the human condition is the Author of mankind, our Creator, God. Do not discount the value of seeking the highest counsel of all.

Realize the answer to your control lies in your mind. Refuse failure, seek the counsel of experts, practice until it's a part of who you are and then begin to expect success and control.

ACTION POINTS

1. Realize that a lack of control can destroy your career or life.

2. Is there and area of your life that you cannot seem to control?

3. What do you do to combat your lack of control in this area?

4. Do you avoid placing yourself in situations where you are vulnerable to this issue?

5. Employ the power of your mind to combat control issues. Do you program you mind with constructive thoughts?

6. Seek the counsel and advice of experts. Do not discount the counsel of the highest of them all.

7. Who can you turn to for counsel?

8. Refuse to accept failure as an option!

9. Expect success!

Quotes from Nolan Ryan

"I can't think of anything more humiliating than losing a ballgame to a guy who steals home on you. It happened to me one time against Kansas City. I had a 2-2 count on the hitter - and Amos Otis broke from third. The pitch was a ball and he slid in safe. I felt like a nickel."

"It helps if the hitter thinks you're a little crazy."

"My job is to give my team a chance to win."

"One of the beautiful things about baseball is that every once in a while you come into a situation... where you want to and where you have to... reach down and prove something."

LESSON NINETEEN - DON'T MESS WITH TEX!

It has been said that half of the plate belongs to the hitter and the other half belongs to the pitcher. Conventional wisdom says that the inside part of the plate belongs to the hitter and the outside part of the plate belongs to the pitcher. Don Drysdale who hit 154 batters in his 14-year career said, "That's fine that half of the plate belongs to the hitter and half belongs to me. That's fair. I just never let the hitter know what half is mine."

Nolan Ryan was a pitcher who was also never afraid to brush a hitter back with an inside pitch. And during his 27 year career he hit quite a few batters. However, only two of them had the guts (or foolishness) to charge the Texas sized pitcher. In 1983 Pedro Guerrero of the Los Angeles Dodgers, was hit in the helmet by a Nolan Ryan pitch. He made no attempt to charge the mound. He instead, just happy to be alive, took his place at first base. The ball actually cracked Guerrero's helmet, and after the game he asked Ryan to autograph it.

All hitters were not as forgiving. San Diego Padre, Dave Winfield, responded to being hit by a Nolan Ryan pitch by charging the mound. Ryan covered his pitching arm and dropped to the ground. Not one of Winfield's random punches made significant contact and Ryan escaped with only a bruised ego. However, he was embarrassed by the way he responded. He vowed that if he were ever in the same situation he would defend himself.

Thirteen years went by and it seemed that no batter would dare challenge Ryan to a duel until a moment in a game between the Texas Rangers and the Chicago White Sox. Robin Ventura was grazed by a pitch from Ryan and immediately charged the mound. Ventura ducked his head to barrel into his target. Nolan snared him in a headlock as if he was back on his ranch wrestling a calf. Ryan then landed several solid punches on the top of Ventura's head before they were pulled apart.

Nolan was allowed to stay in the game. However, Ventura was ejected. This moment strengthened Ryan's legend in the admiring eyes of his fans. Ventura, after the game, was asked how he felt that a man twice his age "got the better of him." Although, it would be a hard case to make, he assured everyone that Ryan didn't. Ryan, who was a spokesperson for Advil at the time, was asked about the incident. He quipped, "Just give him a couple of Advil and he will be ready to go another nine innings."

A few years ago, I was at a Texas Rangers baseball game, sitting just below a luxury box that was holding Nolan Ryan. As fate would have it, Robin Ventura came to the plate and was booed by 35,000 fans. The fans hadn't forgotten the assault on their hero five years prior. Quickly the fans switched from boos to chants of "No-lan...No-lan...Nolan."

Ryan made a decision thirteen years prior how he would respond in that situation and he delivered admirably. Ryan could have very easily fallen to the ground like he had done thirteen years before and as has become the norm for pitchers to do. But, Ryan refused to do that. He told himself, "If that situation ever occurs again I will stand my ground and fight." He made a decision to act differently next time. We have to program our minds in advance to react and if we don't, in the heat of the moment, we may not perform in a manner in which we will be proud.

Jerry Parr and Tim McCarthy made such a decision years ago. They decided how they would react in a life or death situation years before the hour presented itself. When it did, their minds instantly overcame the instinct telling them to flee and fall to the ground. Mr. McCarthy and Mr. Parr were secret service agents for Ronald Reagan. When John Hinckley began firing, Parr covered Reagan's body with his and threw him into the limousine. McCarthy stood with his arms outstretched like a wall of granite and took a bullet for the President and the country. Both of these men reacted in a fraction of a second. The only reason they were able to react so rapidly is because they had decided before the event how they would handle themselves if it occurred. They reacted and the nation thanks them with words that pale in comparison to the task they expertly executed.

Decide today how you will perform in the future. If you don't, if you leave it to chance, you might not want to remember it.

Action Points

1. Have you performed below your expectations in an area?

2. How would you have liked to handle that same situation?

3. Perhaps you haven't performed below your expectations in an area. But, what is it that is important to you? What are your goals?

4. How do you see yourself performing when challenges arise?

5. See yourself succeeding in this situation. Visualize how you would like it to occur. Make sure it's real to you. See yourself accomplishing it in vivid detail. Record the rewards of performing in this manner. This is referred to as autosuggestion. Your mind is powerful and if the scenario is vivid and detailed enough your subconscious will assume it as real and store it in your data banks as an appropriate behavior for the future.

"The best possible thing in baseball is winning the World Series. The second best thing is losing the World Series."
Tommy Lasorda

"Don't worry about your individual numbers. Worry about the team. If the team is successful, each of you will be successful, too."
Branch Rickey

"In baseball, you can't kill the clock. You've got to give the other man his chance. That's why this is the greatest game."
Earl Weaver

"Managing is like holding a dove in your hand. Squeeze too hard and you kill it, not hard enough and it flies away."
Tommy Lasorda

"Pitch within yourself."
Tom Seaver

"Associate with those who help you believe in yourself."
Brooks Robinson

"If you get fooled by a pitch with less than two strikes, take it."
Ted Williams

"Be on time. Bust your butt. Play smart. And have some laughs along the way."
Whitey Herzog

"It takes pitching, hitting and defense. Any two can win. All three make you unbeatable."
Joe Garagiola

"If you can't outsmart people, outwork them."
Bill Veeck

"Mental attitude and concentration are the keys to pitching."
Ferguson Jenkins

"Baseball isn't just the stats. As much as anything else, baseball is the style of Willie Mays, or the determination of Hank Aaron, or the endurance of a Mickey Mantle, the discipline of Carl Yastrzemski, the drive of Eddie Mathews, the reliability of a (Al) Kaline or a (Joe) Morgan, the grace of a (Joe) DiMaggio, the kindness of a Harmon Killebrew, and the class of Stan Musial, the courage of a Jackie Robinson, or the heroism of Lou Gehrig. My hope for the game is that these qualities will never be lost."
President George W. Bush

"You don't have to weigh 250 pounds to make good in baseball and you don't have to be six-foot-seven either. I like that. I was a little fellow myself."
President Harry Truman

"You know how I really feel? I feel like a baseball team going into the ninth inning with only eight men left to play."
President Franklin Roosevelt

"Not making the baseball team at West Point was one of the greatest disappointments of my life, maybe my greatest."
President Dwight D. Eisenhower

"We cheer for the Senators, we pray for the Senators, and we hope that the Supreme Court does not declare that unconstitutional."
President Lyndon Johnson

"Fundamentals are the most valuable tools a player can possess. Bunt the ball into the ground. Hit the cutoff man. Take the extra base. Learn the fundamentals"
Dick Williams

"A hitter's impatience is the pitcher's biggest advantage."
Pete Rose

"Good fielding and pitching, without hitting, or vice versa, is like Ben Franklin's half pair of scissors--ineffectual."
Moe Berg

"The pitcher has to throw a strike sooner or later, so why not hit the pitch you want to hit and not the one he wants you to hit?"
Johnny Mize

"Players who commit errors need reassurance from the pitcher, who must harbor no grudges."
Roger Craig

"Control is what kept me in the big leagues for twenty-two years."
Cy Young

Quotes about Christy Matthewson

"Mathewson pitched against Cincinnati yesterday. Another way of putting it is that Cincinnati lost a game of baseball. The first statement means the same as the second."
Damon Runyon

"Mathewson was the greatest pitcher who ever lived. He had knowledge, judgment, perfect control and form. It was wonderful to watch him pitch when he wasn't pitching against you."
Connie Mack

Matthewson—N. Y. Nat.

Lesson Twenty - Was He Safe?

The ball is hit deep in the hole at first. The pitcher races the runner to the bag. The pitcher takes the toss from the first baseman and quickly tags the bag with his foot. It's a close play. It's a very close play. The umpire is motionless and the crowd waits for his reaction. The umpire turns to the pitcher and says, "Was he safe or out?" The pitcher replies in a certain tone, "He was out!" "All right then," the umpire exclaims, "Your're out!" With no argument the runner trots to his dug out and play resumes.

Does this sound like a far-fetched scenario? It does to me and I doubt it ever happened. However, rumor has it that there was once a player who was so respected around the league that umpires sometimes asked him his opinion on close plays. Personally, I believe this is an example of a phrase getting whispered in an ear and then getting distorted as it's passed along the gossip and legend trail. However, the rumor most likely had its birth in truth. And that truth is that you can trust Christy Matthewson.

Christy Matthewson entered the Major Leagues at the age of nineteen and played for the Giants. In his first full season, he won twenty games with an ERA of 2.41. He was a 6'1 blond-hair and blue-eyed son of a prosperous farmer. His humility and honesty were traits that he soon became known by. You will often find the word "gentleman" associated with Christy Matthewson. "Matthewson altered turn of the century conceptions about men who played the game," wrote Tom Meany of the New York World Telegram. "Through him, the public learned that a professional ballplayer doesn't need to be a hayseed or a tough-talking, tobacco-chewing, whiskey-guzzling refugee from the pool rooms of the teeming cities."

Matthewson played seventeen seasons and almost all of them for New York. He ended his career with a 2.13 ERA, 2,502 strikeouts, 373 wins and only 188 losses. He led the league in ERA's two seasons, posted 37 wins in 1908 and played in a total of 635 games. He threw a pitch he referred to as his "fade away" that truly baffled National League hitters. He is remembered as one of the game's best pitchers, but perhaps more importantly he is remembered as a man of character. There's that word again...character. What does character mean? Webster defines character as "moral strength." I like that definition. Character is equated with strength.

In 635 contests Matthewson was never thrown out of a game. Why? He was a cool headed ballplayer and man. Matthewson served in World War I and was gassed in a training exercise. He contracted tuberculosis and died seven years later. His death was announced before the 1925 World Series and players on both sides wore black arm bands. Matthewson had gained the respect of his peers. One hundred years after he began his career, he is still known for his honesty, cool headedness and gentlemanly behavior.

Did umpires really ask Matthewson for his advice on calls? Probably not. However, Matthewson conducted himself in a manner that led everyone to respect him. Where does respect come from? It doesn't come with a title. You can't assign leadership or respect by assigning a title. It comes from consistency. You can't be a leader today and a whiner tomorrow and be a leader the day after. It's about consistency. This weekend, I attended a church function and listened in awe as I watched a man sing some of the most heart felt religious songs I have ever heard. In an instant my mind made an impression of this man as a leader. Afterwards, in a three-minute conversation, he tore that tower of respect and leadership down with careless off color jokes. When I left I assessed that he was a gifted singer, but not the leader I had guessed.

Printing "President" or "South Area Vice President" on your business card won't garner respect. However, by playing in 635 games with quiet politeness and honesty you will. Don't try to assign respect...earn it.

ACTION POINTS

1. Are you trusted?

2. How do you know?

3. How are you attempting to assign respect to yourself?

4. What can you do to stop trying to assign respect and start earning it?

5. In what areas do you need to work on the character quality of honesty?

Quotes from Whitey Herzog

"A sense of humor and a good bullpen."
(needs for successful manager)

"Baseball has been good to me since I quit trying to play it."

"Down there (New Athens, Illinois), we've got more taverns than grocery stores. I walked in, threw down a bill and said, 'Give everybody a drink.' Nice gesture I thought, but down the bar somebody yelled, 'Hey big shot, your brother is still a better ballplayer than you are.'"

Herzog's Rules
1. Be on time.
2. Bust your butt.

3. Play smart.
4. Have some laughs while you're at it.
"If you don't have outstanding relief pitching, you might as well piss on the fire and call the dogs."

"The only thing bad about winning the pennant is that you have to manage the All-Star Game the next year. I'd rather go fishing for three years."

"The rules are changed now, there's not any way to build a team today. It's just how much money you want to spend. You could be the world champions and somebody else makes a key acquisition or two and you're through."
Quotes from Dizzy Dean

"All ballplayers want to wind up their careers with the Cubs, Giants or Yankees. They just can't help it."

"Anybody who's ever had the privilege of seeing me play knows that I am the greatest pitcher in the world."

"He (Bill Terry) once hit a ball between my legs so hard that my center-fielder caught it on the fly backing up against the wall."

"He slid into third."

"If Satch (Paige) and I were pitching on the same team, we would clinch the pennant by July fourth and go fishing until World Series time."

"I know who's the best pitcher I ever seen and it's old Satchel Paige, that big lanky colored boy. My fastball looks like a change of pace alongside that little pistol bullet old Satchel shoots up to the plate." - Sport (1969)

"It ain't braggin' if you can back it up."

"Let the teachers teach English and I will teach baseball. There is a lot of people in the United States who say isn't, and they ain't eating."

Quotes from Mickey Mantle

"After I hit a home run I had a habit of running the bases with my head down. I figured the pitcher already felt bad enough without me showing him up rounding the bases."

"All I had was natural ability."

"All the ballparks and the big crowds have a certain mystique. You feel attached, permanently wedded to the sounds that ring out, to the fans chanting your name, even when there are only four or five thousand in the stands on a Wednesday afternoon."

"A lot of people wrote that Roger (Maris) and I didn't like each other and that we didn't get along. Nothing could be further from the truth."

"A team is where a boy can prove his courage on his own. A gang is where a coward goes to hide."

"As far as I'm concerned, Aaron is the best ball player of my era. He is to baseball of the last fifteen years what Joe DiMaggio was before him. He's never received the credit he's due."

"To think you're a .300 hitter and end up at .237 in your last season, then find yourself looking at a lifetime .298 average - it made me want to cry."

LESSON TWENTY ONE - ERRORS THAT DON'T HURT?

How many times have you witnessed this scenario?

There are two outs and a runner on first. The ball is hit for an easy out to the short stop and he boots the ball. Everyone watches hopelessly as the ball rolls into center field and everyone is safe. The defensive team has given the offense an extra out. The pitcher bears down and looks intensely at the signs. The call is for a pitch low and away. He hits his mark for strike one. Two pitches later "strike three" is called and the batter tosses his helmet in disgust as the position players trot to the dugout.

Many times the announcer will happily shout into the microphone that, "Despite the error no damage was done and we head to the ninth with the score still 3-2!" Oh really? No damage was done? Yes, it's true that no feet crossed the plate and the score remained intact despite the error. However, I don't believe the argument can be made that 100% of the time no damage is done.

I remember watching a playoff game in 1999 and the baseball genius, Joe Morgan, made this point. He explained that what the error did was allow everyone in the lineup to, in his words, "Get closer to their next at bat." You see, there is someone who wasn't going to leadoff the next inning who now will because of the error. There is someone that may not have gotten another chance at the plate who now will. Perhaps the cleanup hitter will get another at bat the next inning that could have been avoided.

Errors are just that, errors. And they all count. They all change the outcome of the game. Many times the error can be minimized and the inning, and eventually the game, can be secured despite the error. However, the error did, even if just a little, shake the game from its track and in some way effect its outcome. Attention to detail and preparation can help prevent frequent errors. However, it will not stop them altogether. They will occur. When they do, ask yourself what led to the error and how you can correct it next time. Don't just brush over it thinking "the error did no damage."

Am I suggesting that you should dwell on your errors? Absolutely not. One ingredient that makes professional athletes stand out from the thousands of talented men who did not make it to the Major Leagues is their mental toughness. It's the ability to forget about the error and focus on the next play. The time to analyze an error is not in the midst of competition, rather it is from the rest and comfort of retrospection. Do not dwell on errors. Instead, analyze and correct. Dwelling on errors will only lead to future errors, and I hope we all understand that future errors are damaging even if no one scores.

ACTION POINTS

1. Take errors seriously because every error changes the game.

2. Take all steps to "forget the error" and mentally focus on what is happening now.

3. Practice, practice, practice to keep errors at a minimum.

4. Set aside a time after the event has occurred to review your successes and errors.

5. In an objective and unattached approach probe yourself to what caused the miscue and how you could prevent it.

6. What are some errors or mistakes that you often let "slide" because you don't see the impact?

7. Baseball is a routine game and the team that makes the routine plays usually wins.

Quotes from Sandy Koufax

"I can't believe that Babe Ruth was a better player than Willie Mays. Ruth is to baseball what Arnold Palmer is to golf. He got the game moving. But I can't believe he could run as well as Mays, and I can't believe he was any better an outfielder."

"If I could straighten it out (his golf swing), I'd be pitching at Dodger Stadium tonight."

"If there was any magic formula, it was getting to pitch every fourth day."

LESSON TWENTY TWO - WHAT'S YOUR EXCUSE?

In doing my research for this book, I stumbled across this story and I couldn't help but smile. I think I even chuckled. There were several lessons that I could have chosen for number twenty-two. However, I just couldn't leave this one out. It's a truly remarkable story. Our lesson comes to us from a man named Hub Kittle and the feat he accomplished on August 27, 1980.

Hub pitched in a Triple A game against Des Moines. Hub faced four batters and retired them all. With one out in the second inning he was replaced by another pitcher. What is the big deal you say? Good question. It's this, Hub was born in 1917! That's right. He pitched in a Triple A game in August 1980 and was born in 1917. That made him 63 years old when he took the mound!

Hub Kittle wrote a letter to Seth Swirsky for Seth to include in his book, "Every Pitcher Tells a Story." If you love baseball get that book!

Hub wrote:
"One day, A. Ray Smith, the owner of the Springfield team, where I was pitching coach, asked me if I would pitch as a promotion. 'Sure' I says, not really taking him seriously. I was 63 and a half years old at the time!

A few weeks later, I was up in the press box and all the reporters up there they says, 'Hey Hub, did you know that you are going to start tomorrow night?' I said 'What!?' I walked into the office and Alice, the owner's secretary, handed me a contract to sign for $1. So I signed it. The next night we had a game against a triple A team in Des Moines. I warmed up in the bullpen, felt pretty good.

I looked down at the first batter and I swear to God he looked like he was two miles away. He looked so small. I was used to throwing B.P. (batting practice) up in front of the rubber all the time and now I had to throw it what seemed like a mile. So I says to myself, 'What are you doing here you dumb, dumb, dumb donkey?'

I took my wind up off the first hitter and I will be damned if he didn't try to bunt the ball off me. The ball went foul and I said to him as he went by 'with the next pitch you are going down on your gazaba, boy!' Next pitch I put right under his chin. All the fans clapped like hell. I got him out and got the next two hitters plus the first hitter in the next inning and that was that...."

Did you smile while reading that letter? Me too. So here's the question. What's your excuse? Seriously, what's your excuse? You may say, "My excuse for what?" What is your excuse for not doing everything that you are capable of, your excuse for not living your dream, your excuse for not chasing your goal, your excuse for not being the best that you can be?

I don't mean to be harsh. If you are reading this book, I know something very important about you. You are someone who strives to improve themselves, therefore, you are already moving in the right direction. However, is there something you would really love to do and you are not chasing that goal because you are too old, too young, too tall, too short, don't have the money, have too much money, don't have the time or aren't smart enough? Folks, Hub proved to us that amazing things can be accomplished at any age. Don't let your excuses stop you from chasing your goals.

Hub could have very easily said, "No, I am too old to pitch." But, he didn't. He risked looking like a fool and came out looking like a hero. Thanks for the lesson, Hub. I saved the best for last.

ACTION POINTS

1. What is your excuse?

2. What would you like to be doing but have put it off because of a self-imposed excuse?

3. What can you do today to move towards your goal?

REVIEW

1. Which Success Lesson(s) stood out to you the most?

2. Why? What did that lesson(s) teach you?

3. What are your goals for the next year?

4. The next 2 years?

5. The next 5 years?

6. For your life?

I look forward to seeing you at the ballpark! You may contact me directly at www.ronwhitetraining.com.

Baseball Facts

Major League umpire Cal Hubbard is the only person in both the baseball and football hall of fame.

The average life of a Major League baseball is seven pitches.

Before 1859, baseball umpires were seated in padded chairs behind home Plate.

The only two days of the year in which there are no professional sports games (MLB, NBA, NHL, or NFL) are the day before and the day after the Major League All-Star Game.

The silhouette on the Major League Baseball logo is Harmon Killebrew.

A forfeited game in baseball is recorded as a 9-0 score.

Cy Young won more games than anyone in Major League history yet never won the Cy Young award! (I will let you think about that.)

John Lee Richmond pitched the first perfect game on June 12, 1880.

William Howard Taft was the first president to throw out a pitch in a baseball game.

The first television broadcast of a Major League baseball game was between the Cincinnati Reds and the Brooklyn Dodgers on August 26, 1939.

The candy bar, Baby Ruth, is named after the daughter of President Cleveland, not Babe Ruth, the baseball player as most think.

Hank Aaron's 715th home run. Pitcher: Al Downing. The outfielder who climbed the fence in a vain attempt to catch the ball: Bill Buckner. Who caught the ball? Tom House, relief pitcher for Atlanta.

The most pitches ONE pitcher can throw to ONE batter in ONE at-bat with no foul balls and still strike him out is 11. How? The count is 2-and-2 (4 pitches) there is a runner on base. On the 3-2 pitch (pitch 5) the runner is thrown out trying to steal for the third out of the inning. The same batter starts the next inning with a new count, which he strikes out on 6 pitches (3 balls 3 strikes for a total of 11 pitches in all).

Lou Gehrig began his consecutive game streak by batting for Pee-Wee Wanninger the day before he subbed for ailing first baseman, Wally Pipp.

George Kell of the 1945 Athletics went 0-for-10 in a 24-inning game. His lifetime average, though, was .306.

The 1990 New York Yankee pitching staff set an all-time record with the fewest complete games, three.

The unassisted triple play has been turned in regular season Major League play only eleven times in this century and just one questionable time in the nineteenth. (It also happened once in World Series play.)

Steve Carlton is the only pitcher to win a Cy Young with a last place team, the '72 Phillies. He went 27-10 on a team that only won 56 games.

Babe Ruth wore a cabbage leaf under his cap while playing baseball, and he used to change it every 2 innings.

After 43 years of losing, Charlie Brown actually won a baseball game on March 30, 1993.

When baseball was first beginning, the pitcher's mound was only 45 feet from home plate. It used to take 8 balls to walk somebody. If a person hit the ball and it bounced once and someone caught the ball, the person that hit it would be called out. Walks also used to be counted as base hits.

The first five inductees to the Baseball Hall of Fame were Babe Ruth (P/RF), Ty Cobb (CF), Walter Johnson (P), Christy Mathewson (P), and Honus Wagner (SS).

Until the year 1999, there were four red numerals inside separate white baseball banners hung in right field at Fenway Park. They represented the numbers the Red Sox had retired over the years, in order of the player's retirement. Ted Williams was first (#9), Bobby Doerr second (#4), Johnny Pesky third (#1), and Carl Yastrzemski last (#8). Ironically; however, those four numbers in the order they were in, 9-4-1-8, also represented September 4th 1918, the date on which the Red Sox won their last World Series title. The numbers were rearranged in sequential order (1-4-8-9) when Fenway was repainted before the All-Star game.

The Official Rules of Major League Baseball say in section 1.04a that "any playing field constructed by a professional club after June 1,1958, shall provide a minimum distance of 325 feet from home base to the nearest fence, stand or other obstruction on the right and left field foul lines." Minute Maid Field in Houston and Pac Bell Park in San Francisco, constructed in 1999, both have fences only 315 feet from home plate to the right and left field lines, respectively.

Rookies (players in their first year) are named after the rook in chess. Rooks generally are the last pieces to be moved into action, and the same goes for Rookies.

The only logo not allowed on a Major League baseball uniform is a baseball.

Daryll Strawberry is the only player to play for all four teams that originated in New York: Yankees, Dodgers, Giants and Mets.

Rip Collins constructed a picket fence in front of his house from his broken bats.

The 1945 Senators did not hit one home run over the fence at home. They did, however, have one inside the park home run at home that year.

1899 Cleveland Spiders, a National League entry, won 20 games and lost 134 for a .130 "winning" percentage.

While hitting 61 homers for the New York Yankees during the 1961 season, Roger Maris never received an intentional walk; Mickey Mantle was hitting behind him.

In 1960, the Cleveland Indians and Detroit Tigers traded managers in midseason. Both teams were going nowhere at the time of the trade and nothing changed afterwards.

Connie Mack spent 50 seasons as the manager of the Philadelphia Athletics. He retired at age 88.

Babe Ruth wore the number three because he was batting third in the lineup at the time the team added numbers to their uniforms. Lou Gehrig, who batted behind him, drew number four.

Ray Chapman died from a pitch by Carl Mays during a game in 1920 and is the only Major League player ever killed on the diamond.

In 1973 Norm Cash tried to break up a Nolan Ryan no hitter with a table leg. Cash came to the plate with the sawed-off leg of an old table in the club house.

Johnny Mize is the only player to have at least 50 homers but less than 50 strikeouts in the same season. He had 51 homers and 42 strikeouts in the 1947 season.

Stan Williams was known as the "Big Hurt" long before Frank Thomas was pegged with the name. He got the nickname during his first trip with the team- when he accidentally spiked barefoot Mickey Mantle in an adjacent toilet stall.

Bobo Holloman no-hit the Philadelphia Athletics in his starting debut May 6, 1953. But, he never pitched another complete game in the majors.

Joel Niekro hit his only Major League homer against his brother Phil in a 1976 game. Together, the Niekro's won more games (539) than any pair of pitching brothers.

STRANGE BUT TRUE
BASEBALL INJURIES

Indians reliever, Paul Shuey, sustained a knot in his shoulder when he fell asleep holding his baby.

Ruben Sierra sprained his ankle while chasing his daughter on a mall escalator.

Royals outfielder Mark Quinn cracked a rib while kung-fu fighting with his brother.

Wade Boggs injured his back while putting on his cowboy boots.

George Brett broke his toe on a chair in his home while running to watch Bill Buckner hit.

Tony Gwynn fractured his finger when he slammed the door of his Porsche on his hand.

In 1998, Arizona Diamondbacks pitcher, Brian Anderson, burned his face with a steam iron in his hotel room. He was attempting to simulate the heat he would face in his next outing in Texas.

Rickey Henderson sat out for a weekend in August due to frostbite on his foot from a synthetic ice pack.

In 1996, Cal Ripken suffered a broken nose while posing for a picture for the American League All-Star team photo. White Sox pitcher Roberto Hernandez accidentally struck Ripken while stumbling off the platform.

Before game 4 of the 1985 NLCS, Cardinals outfielder Vince Coleman got run over by a tarp machine and missed the playoffs. Later, as a New York Met, he accidentally struck teammate Doc Gooden with a 9-iron while practicing his swing in the clubhouse.

In 1986, Ranger pitcher Charlie Hough, broke his little finger on his pitching hand, while shaking hands.

July 14, 1914, Giants outfielder Red Murray was hit by lightening as he catches the final out in a 21 inning marathon against the Pirates.

Although he is knocked unconscious, there appears to be no permanent harm done.

Rangers pitcher, Paul Kilgus, strained his back while hugging his wife upon his team's return from training camp.

In 1990, Blue Jays outfielder Glenallen Hill landed on the DL after jumping through a glass table, suffering multiple cuts and carpet burns. He had a nightmare that spiders were attacking him.

In 1946, the Senator's George Myatt tripped on the dugout steps and broke his ankle - while attempting to take the field for the season opener.

During the 1950s, Cleveland's Luke Easter leaped to cheer a teammate, hit his head on the dugout roof and was knocked unconscious.

Pitcher Bob Newsom broke a leg getting kicked at a mule auction.

After hearing a motivational speech, Brewers knuckleballer Steve Sparks tried to tear a telephone book in half and dislocated his shoulder.

After throwing a New Years Eve party in 1992, Cardinals pitcher Joe Magrane saw a seven of clubs on his ceiling. Apparently, it was left by the magician he had hired. While trying to retrieve the card, Magrane fell from a ladder and broke his heel.

Braves pitcher, Cecil Upshaw, injured his finger on a street sign while showing his friends how he once dunked in the NBA.

In 1982 Kirk Gibson, pulled a stool from under Tigers teammate Dave Rozema. Unfortunately, Rozema had a bottle of cough syrup in his pocket and sustained a lacerated rear end.

Ron White, Memory and Sales Training Expert, has since 1991, been in the training and personal development industry. He has delivered workshops for Boy Scouts of America, The United States Army, Ford, Century 21, Norwest Mortgage, Coldwell Banker, Chevrolet, Sprint, Merrill Lynch and thousands more across the country.

Ron has studied human development, the mental process and the power of a trained mind. Using techniques he's perfected, he broke a World Record for memory by memorizing a 28-digit number in one minute, 15 seconds, he's been the guest on over 50 radio programs and has appeared on US and British television discussing memory enhancement!

Ron is the author of two books and multiple CD programs including his best-selling, Memory in a Month program, Speed Reading, Write It On Your Heart, and How to Develop the Mind of Einstein.

For More Information or to Schedule Ron White to speak at your next event...

Contact: **YourSuccessStore.com**
(877) 929-0439
(817) 442-8549 (local or international)
2835 Exchange Blvd., Suite 200
Southlake, TX 76092
speaker@yoursuccessstore.com

Ron's Most Popular Training Topics:

- How to Have a Winning Year
- Improve Your Memory - Double Your Sales
- The Benefits of a Powerful Memory
- 22 Success Lessons from Baseball
- How to Develop the Mind of Einstein
- Selling's Not Telling

A word from Ron White:

"This seminar is going to be fun, it is going to be professional and it is going to be educational. Your group is going to be laughing and they are going to have a great time. But they will also walk away with some very tangible skills that they can put into practice that day to increase their productivity and to increase their performance.

This seminar will be one you will never forget. Please call or email and let's schedule this wonderful opportunity for your group today.

Ron White

Scheduling Ron to speak at your next event is a ***sure home run!***

Additional Products by Ron White

MEMORY IN A MONTH
6 CD's and Guide Book
In only 10 minutes a day, for 30 consecutive days, you can transform your mind from forgetful to unbelievable!

WRITE IT ON YOUR HEART
2 CD's and Workbook
Memorize scripture and experience the life change that results when the Word of God is written on your heart.

SPEED READING - 4 CD's and Workbook
Speed Reading is an extremely comprehensive program and covers everything from the very basics of speed reading to building your vocabulary and remembering what you read.

HOW TO DEVELOP THE MIND OF EINSTEIN - 6 CD's
This program will entertain you *and* it will give you strategies and ideas on how to improve your thinking, skills, relationships and time management.

---

22 Success Lessons from Baseball by Ron White

To order copies of this book for yourself or your organization, please see quantity discounts below:
(Retail $12.95)

1-9	$9.00 ea
10-24	$7.00 ea
25-99	$4.50 ea
100+	$3.00 ea

To order call 877-929-0439 or visit www.YourSuccessStore.com

Over 200 titles available including:

CD/VIDEO/DVD

Winning with Influence – Chris Widener (8 CDs)
Psychology of Winning – Dennis Waitley (6 CDs)
Secrets of Closing the Sale – Zig Ziglar (12 CDs)
The Psychology of Selling – Brian Tracy (6 CDs)
Raising Positive Kids in a Negative World – Zig Ziglar (6 CDs)
The Art of Exceptional Living – Jim Rohn (6 CDs)
The Best of Connie Podesta "Live" – Connie Podesta (6 CDs)
How to Have Your Best Year Ever – Jim Rohn (1 DVD)
Memory in a Month – Ron White (6 CDs wkbk)

TRAINING PACKAGES

The Platinum Collection - Denis Waitley (18 CDs)
Success Mastery Academy - Brian Tracy (16 CDs/workbook)
2004 Jim Rohn Weekend Event (12 DVDs, 24 CDs plus 283-page wkbk)
The Complete How to Stay Motivated Package - Zig Ziglar (3 Volumes plus Performance Planner)
Ron White Training Packages (see page 127)
and Many More...

Order by mail, phone or fax.
Payment: Check,
Mastercard, Visa,
AmEx or Discover

SHIPPING & HANDLING

For orders .... Please Add
Up to $24.99 .... $5.95
$25 to $74.99 .... $6.95
$75 to $149.99 .... $7.95
$150 to $349.99 ..... $9.95
Over $350 .... 3% of order

Applies to US orders sent UPS Ground. Call for quotes on International and overnight shipping.

Mix and Match Pricing
on Zig Ziglar, Jim Rohn, Denis Waitley
and Brian Tracy Excerpt Booklets

	Regular	20% OFF
1	$1.50 each	$1.30 each
2-9	$1.25 each	$1.00 each
10-24	$1.00 each	$.80 each
25-99	$.90 each	$.72 each
100-599	$.80 each	$.64 each
600-1199	$.65 each	$.52 each
1200+	$.60 each	$.48 each

All prices are in U.S. Dollars.

For product orders, seminar schedules, or corporate speaking inquiries please contact:

www.YourSuccessStore.com
Sign up for FREE - YSS Achievement Ezine
Best-selling books, CDs , DVDs, MP3s and ebooks by:

- **Jim Rohn**
- **Zig Ziglar**
- **Brian Tracy**
- **Ron White**
- **Les Brown**
- **Denis Waitley**
- **Connie Podesta**
- **Chris Widener**

2835 Exchange Blvd., Ste. 200, Southlake, TX 76092
(877) 929-0439   (817) 442-8549   FAX (817) 442-1390